PROCEEDINGS OF THE INTERNATIONAL
GERMAN ALUMNI SUMMER SCHOOL PROGRAM

6–14 October 2018

I0131846

PROCEEDINGS OF THE INTERNATIONAL GERMAN ALUMNI SUMMER
SCHOOL PROGRAM

6–14 October 2018

Education, Science and Cooperation for Sustainable Development and Biodiversity Conservation

Edited by

Martin Kappas, Margaretha Pangau-Adam, Jolanta Slowik, Peninah Aloo

Photo on the front cover by Rindrahatsarana Ramanankirahina

Supported by

DAAD Deutscher Akademischer Austausch Dienst
German Academic Exchange Service

Bibliographical information held by the German National Library

The German National Library has listed this book in the Deutsche Nationalbibliografie (German national bibliography); detailed bibliographic information is available online at http://dnb.d-nb.de.

1st edition - Göttingen: Cuvillier, 2019

© CUVILLIER VERLAG, Göttingen, Germany 2019
Nonnenstieg 8, 37075 Göttingen, Germany
Telephone: +49 (0)551-54724-0
Telefax: +49 (0)551-54724-21
www.cuvillier.de

1st edition, 2019

This publication is printed on acid-free paper.

ISBN 978-3-7369-9984-8
eISBN 978-3-7369-8984-9

ACKNOWLEDGEMENTS

We would like to thank the German Academic Exchange Service (DAAD) for providing the financial support in publishing this Proceedings. We would also like to express our sincere thanks to the Georg-August University of Göttingen (GAUG), Germany, especially to Prof. Dr. Martin Kappas, the head of Department of Cartography, GIS and Remote Sensing, University of Göttingen and the organizer team for giving extensive support and cooperation in a successful implementation of the International Summer School. We are very thankful to the Leadership of Karatina University Kenya, in particular Prof. Dr. Peninah Aloo and Dr. Mugo Mware (Faculty of Natural Resources and Environmental Studies) and the University staff for the cooperation and assistance, and the great hospitality during the summer school. Sincere gratitude is also expressed to all the invited speakers, experts, participants, students and all organizations for their active contribution in this scientific activity.

CONTENTS

INTRODUCTION

Education, Science and Cooperation for Sustainable Development and Biodiversity Conservation in Africa

The German Alumni Summer School 2018 on 'Education, science and cooperation between German Alumni for sustainable development and biodiversity conservation in Sub-Saharan Africa' was jointly organized by the Faculty of Geography-Department of Cartography, GIS and Remote Sensing, the Faculty of Biology and Psychology-Department of Conservation Biology, and the Karatina University, Kenya – School of Natural Resources and Environmental Studies. This summer school was funded by the German Academic Exchange Service (DAAD) and targeted to the German Alumni from Sub-Saharan Africa as well as scientist and experts from various discipline.

The European Union being confronted with mass migration from Sub-Saharan Africa is currently working on a new political and economic strategy for Africa. Moreover German Government initiated and proposed a new level of equal cooperation between Africa and western countries in areas such as education, trade, business development and energy. The main idea is to limit the effects of climate change and avoid climate refugees, to prevent mass migration and to help create a future for Africa's youth', and underscores the current status and efforts of German development policy towards African countries.

Sub-Saharan Africa comprises of 49 states with the highest population growth, and by the end of the 21st century the population is likely to triple. The average economic growth rate for Sub-Saharan Africa countries slowed down from 5.1% in 2010 to 1.4 % in 2016. Africa is still the world's poorest continent and widespread poverty is the primary cause of malnutrition and health problems. Catastrophes like famines and the recent hunger in Horn of Africa are additionally induced through climate change and land grabbing. Corruption, armed conflict, political and ethnic tension, terrorist activities, unstable state structures, national debt, dependence on global commodities markets, and inequitable world trade mechanisms are mainly responsible for this unstable and threatening situation. Biodiversity loss and diminishing of African wildlife due to habitat loss and poaching are as well the serious concern and calls for action.

It is a fundamental approach to encourage and mobilize the German Alumni in African countries to create significant contribution in sustainable development of this continent.

Higher education is recognised as a powerful tool in promoting sustainable development through integration of principles and practices of sustainable development into all aspects of education and learning. The role of higher education in societies in general and for local or ethnic communities in particular is necessary and crucial for the future of Africa. Implementation of the UNO 2030 Agenda and its 17 Sustainable Development Goals (SDG) for sustainable development involves creation of economic progress in harmony with social justice and in accordance with the earth's ecological limits. The education of African elites, collaborations between German and African Universities and creation of professional networking groups to promote sustainable development, and establishment of joint education and research programs are essential for realization of 2030 Agenda development goals. The Alumni Summer School provided a platform to researchers, academicians, practitioners and entrepreneurs in Sub Sahara African developing countries to share their knowledge and experiences from diverse disciplines ranging from natural and social sciences to humanities with the emphasis on the related-themes and topics of interdisciplinary approach.

The International Summer School aimed to set as a goal, the promotion of sustainable development through higher education, cooperation between Universities and the strengthening of both local and international professional links between the German Alumni. The actual topics dealing with assumptions and difficulties in the identification, categorization and implementation of sustainable development were on the priority agenda. Thereby the competences of alumni for solving socio-economically and environmentally relevant problems have been discussed and expanded.

Capacity building of Alumni were worked out to enhance and upgrade to the latest state of knowledge and expertise for supporting and realizing the UNO 2030 Agenda and its 17 Sustainable Development Goals (SDG). The expertise of the Alumni have been exercised to enable their capabilities for enacting an active role play in their respective home countries as multipliers for knowledge and skill transfer. This will additionally facilitate to restructure their respective universities' curricula and students training for sustainable development, thus may imply the creation of economic progress in harmony with social justice and in accordance with the essential earth's ecological limits which faced by the human beings to date.

With the objectives of discussing the impact of climate change and biodiversity loss on human livelihood, and seeking solutions for sustainable development, the following main areas were covered:

- Global climate change as the challenge for the future
- Challenges and prospects of environmental management and conservation
- Earth observation and Geographical Information Systems (GIS) for Sustainable development
- The role of science and education in nature conservation
- The Relationship between the green concept and global climate change
- Sustainable biodiversity conservation and the benefit to local communities
- Land use changes and impacts on ecosystem services.

NOTE: The contents of the manuscripts are entirely the copyrights of the authors. The Editorial Committee is not responsible for the contents of the publications. Some papers presented at the Summer School are not included for publication in this Proceedings issue as the authors chose not to provide a paper.

Earth Observation and Geographical Information Systems (GIS) for Sustainable Development

MARTIN KAPPAS

Institute of Geography, Georg-August University, Göttingen

Email: mkappas@gwdg.de

Abstract

Earth Information nowadays is able to deliver key information and build up basic knowledge in the fields of Agriculture and Rural development; Water Resources management; Urban Development, Marine Resources, Risk management and Disaster Reduction; Forest Management; Ecosystem Services and Climate Resilience. Finally, Earth Observation delivers data that help to enable a more integrated view on our landscape or in short Remote Sensing and GIS are modern tools inside a more Landscape oriented Approach. The Landscape Approach is about balancing competing land use demands in a way that is best for human well-being and the environment. It means creating solutions that consider food and livelihoods, finance, rights, restoration and progress towards climate and development goals. The presentation is delivering case studies about EO-based information solutions to support targeted environmental problems. It summarizes the importance and applicability of geographic data for sustainable development and draws on experiences in African countries to examine how future sources and applications of geographic data could provide reliable support to decision-makers as they work towards sustainable development. The potential of new technologies, such as satellite remote-sensing systems and geographic information systems, that have revolutionized data collection and analysis over the last decade are explained with a focus on the new Copernicus initiative of the European Space Agency (ESA). EO4SD an ESA initiative to support the uptake of EO-derived information in sustainable development will be shortly presented.

Background information – Identification of national land use challenges Africa / Kenya

While much is known about Africa's biodiversity and nature's contributions to people, there are still significant scientific uncertainties that need to be addressed through national and regional research programmes. The major challenges of national land use problems in Kenia are the following topics:

1. Habitat fragmentation/loss of biodiversity

2. Forest degradation

3. Loss of soil fertility

4. Overgrazing / free grazing

5. Deforestation

6. Soil erosion

7. Siltation and sedimentation of waterbodies

8. Water stress (on water bodies and soils)

9. Flooding

10. Landslides

11. Climate change

All of these 11 topics can be analysed wih the help of GIS and Remote Sensing techniques. Additionally to these 11 topics we find a major thread by Africa's popoulation development. Africa's current population of 1.25 billion is likely to double by 2050, putting severe pressure on the continent's biodiversity and nature's contributions to people, unless appropriate policies and strategies are adopted and effectively implemented. Africa is also one of the most rapidly urbanizing continents. The major challenge for Africa is that the population of Africa surpassed one billion people in 2009 and is set to grow at 2.3 per cent every year during 2010–2015 (World Bank 2011). This means, 2.5 billion people will live in Africa by 2050. In Kenia, we find a 2.6% growth rate / year (2017), which means that Kenia belongs to the fastest growing countries in Africa.

Retrospective to Global Landscapes Forum Nairobi 2018 (UN compound in Nairobi)

The Global Landscapes Forum in Nairobi 2018 is led by the the Center of International Forestry Research (CIFOR) alongside founding partners UN Environment and the World Bank, with core funding provided by the German Government, the Global Landscapes Forum (GLF) accelerates action towards the creation of more resilient, equitable, profitable, productive and healthy landscapes and the achievement of the UNFCCC Paris Agreement and Sustainable Development Goals (Agenda 2030). It is a corner stone for future biodiversity protection. Concerning this important conference some key messages and facts can be summarized:

- Only one fifth of Africa's arable land is under cultivation. (IPBES report, 2018)

- Forests and woodlands make about 23% of Africa's land, while 27% is arable land (IPBES report, 2018)

- In East Africa, some pastoralists, increasingly confined to smaller areas, are forced to keep more animals on degrading pastures or enter conflict with other land users as they move their herds. (FAO, 2015)

- 14.7% of Africa's land is classified as protected. (IPBES report, 2018)

- Africa hosts eight of the world's 36 biodiversity hotpots. (IPBES report, 2018)

- Marine and coastal resources contribute in some African regions to more than 35% of GDP. (IPBES report, 2018)

- By 2100, agricultural gross domestic product (GDP) losses are expected to be greater in West and Central Africa than in North and Southern Africa (0.4%–1.3%). (African Transformation Report, 2017)

- In Africa only about 10 per cent of rural land is registered, with 90 per cent managed informally. (World Bank, 2013)

- Africa counts 369 wetlands of international importance (Ramsar sites), 142 UNESCO World Heritage Sites, 1,255 important bird and biodiversity areas and 158 Alliance for Zero Extinction sites. (IPBES report, 2018)

Finally, we can state that Africa is a biodiversity hotspot under hihg risk. In a short summary the trends / data and projections for Africa are listed (Africa by the numbers):

Trends / data:

- +/- 6.6 million: km2 of land is degraded due to factors such as deforestation, unsustainable agriculture, overgrazing, uncontrolled mining activities, invasive alien species and climate change, leading to soil erosion, salinization, pollution, and loss of vegetation or soil fertility

- +/- 62%: rural population directly dependent on wild nature and its services for survival (the most of any continent)

- +/- 2 million: km2 of land designated as protected (including 6% of biodiversity-rich tropical evergreen broadleaf forests and 2.5% of Africa's seas

- 25%: people having faced hunger and malnutrition (2011–2013) in Sub-Saharan Africa, the world's most food-deficient region

Projections:

- >50% of African bird and mammal species could be lost to climate change by 2100
- 20–30% expected decline in productivity of lakes by 2100
- billion predicted population increase of Africa in 2050 (double the current figure)
- 54%: Africans expected to live in urban and peri-urban areas by 2030 (up from 39% in 2003)

These trends, data and projections shows how much African's biodiversityx is under pressure and that new technologies are needed to sustain African's landscapes. From these trends and projections Africa (esp. Kenia) reacts and postulates certain restoration commitments for the future. A major task in restoration of African landscapes is reforestation. Up to 2018 the following commitments can be listed:

Restoration commitments (status 2018):

- Kenya's National Climate Change Response Strategy calls for growing 7.6 bn trees in the next 20 years. (afr100.org)
- The African Forest Landscape Restoration Initiative (AFR100) aims to restore 100 million hectares of deforested and degraded landscapes across Africa by 2030. (afr100.org)
- The Initiative on Sustainability, Stability and Security in Africa aims to create 2 million green jobs for vulnerable groups through restoration and sustainable land management by 2025. (UNCCD report, 2018, A Rising Africa in a fragile environment)
- Almost $1.5 billion: funds pledged for the AFR100. (afr100.org)
- The Great Green Wall for the Sahara and Sahel, aims to create the planet's larges living structure, stretching on 8,000 km across Africa. (UNCCD)
- The Great Green Wall Initiative aims to capture 250 million tonnes of carbon and create at least 350,000 rural jobs by 2030. (UNCCD)
- More than 8 billion dollars have been mobilized or pledged so far to support the Great Green Wall Initiative. (UNCCD)

An important report about the situation of African's biodiversity is given by the Intergovernmental Platform on Biodiversity and Ecosystem Services (IPBES). This report is an important baseline about the current situation and delivers information such as the most endangered species and their xtinction risk (see Figure 1).

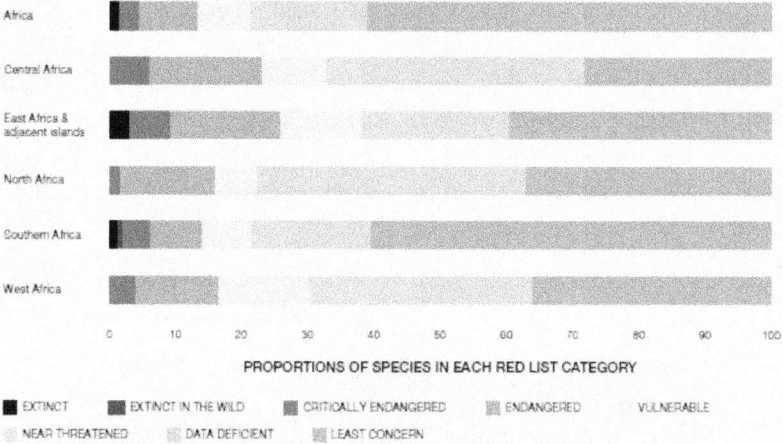

PROPORTIONS OF SPECIES IN EACH RED LIST CATEGORY

- EXTINCT
- EXTINCT IN THE WILD
- CRITICALLY ENDANGERED
- ENDANGERED
- VULNERABLE
- NEAR THREATENED
- DATA DEFICIENT
- LEAST CONCERN

Figure 1. Extinction risk of species endemic to Africa and its subregions (IPBES, 2018)

Figure 1 shows that in East Africa and adjacent islands nearly more than 25% of the species are critically endangerd in the future. Another 10% is vulnerable. In Figrue 2, the key drivers of biodiversity change is shown for the different subregions. For East Africa, we can see that climat change and ilegal wildlife trade have a high impact on biodiversity. On the other side, most oft he protecteted areas of East Africa are under control and need monitoring and control (e.g. with the help of remote sensing technology). Two processes for regional environmental assessment are currently underway:

- the Global Environment Outlook (GEO) and
- Intergovernmental Platform on Biodiversity and Ecosystem Services (IPBES)

Both face constraints of data, time, capacity, and resources and are based on certain knowledge products. As a baseline, three global knowledge products according to their regions and subregions are available as follows:

- The IUCN Red List of Threatened Species,

- Key Biodiversity Areas (specifically Important Bird & Biodiversity Areas [IBAs],
- Protected Planet (Alliance for Zero Extinction [AZE] sites).

These main knowledge products about biodiversity are accompanied by diverse smaller and invidual products (see Figure 3). Another framework for the assessment of biodiversity over Africa is the report "The State of Biodiversity in Africa: A Mid-term Review of Progress towards the Aichi Biodiversity Targets" by United Nations Environment Programme (UNEP). The report identifies opportunities and challenges in implementing the Strategic Plan for Biodiversity 2011–2020 in Africa and looks ahead to actions which need to be taken by national governments and other decision makers to enhance and accelerate progress towards its attainment. Central initiative is the set up of the Aiche biodiversity targets.

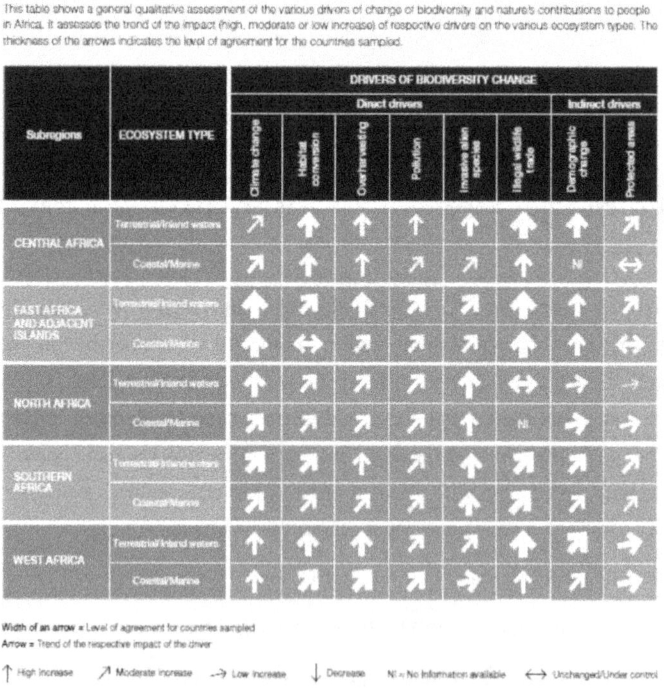

Subregions	Ecosystem type	Climate change	Habitat conversion	Overharvesting	Pollution	Invasive alien species	Illegal wildlife trade	Demographic change	Protected areas
CENTRAL AFRICA	Terrestrial/Inland waters	↗	↑	↑	↑	↑	↑	↑	↗
	Coastal/Marine	↗	↑	↑	↗	↗	↑	NI	↔
EAST AFRICA AND ADJACENT ISLANDS	Terrestrial/Inland waters	↑	↗	↑	↗	↗	↑	↑	↗
	Coastal/Marine	↑	↔	↗	↗	↗	↑	↑	↔
NORTH AFRICA	Terrestrial/Inland waters	↑	↗	↗	↗	↑	↔	→	→
	Coastal/Marine	↗	↗	↗	↗	↑	NI	→	→
SOUTHERN AFRICA	Terrestrial/Inland waters	↗	↗	↑	↗	↑	↗	↗	↗
	Coastal/Marine	↗	↗	↗	↗	↑	↗	↗	↗
WEST AFRICA	Terrestrial/Inland waters	↑	↑	↑	↗	↗	↑	↗	→
	Coastal/Marine	↑	↗	↗	↗	→	↑	↗	→

Figure 2. Key drivers of biodiversity change in Africa shown per subregion and ecosystem type (IPBES, 2018)

File name	Description	Authors	Dryad DOI
Total_Species_GEO.csv	Total numbers of species and of threatened species occurring in each GEO region and subregion	IUCN	http://dx.doi.org/10.5061/dryad.6gb90.2/1.2
Total_Species_IPBES.csv	Total numbers of species and of threatened species occurring in each IPBES region and subregion		http://dx.doi.org/10.5061/dryad.6gb90.2/2.2
Endemic_Species_GEO.csv	Total numbers of species and of threatened species endemic to each GEO region and subregion		http://dx.doi.org/10.5061/dryad.6gb90.2/3.2
Endemic_Species_IPBES.csv	Total numbers of species and of threatened species endemic to each IPBES region and subregion		http://dx.doi.org/10.5061/dryad.6gb90.2/4.2
Red_List_Index_GEO.csv	Relative annual contribution to the global Red List Index for mammals, birds, and amphibians in each GEO region and subregion	IUCN & BirdLife International	http://dx.doi.org/10.5061/dryad.6gb90.2/5.2
Red_List_Index_IPBES.csv	Relative annual contribution to the global Red List Index for mammals, birds, and amphibians in each IPBES region and subregion		http://dx.doi.org/10.5061/dryad.6gb90.2/6.2
IBAs_AZEs_GEO.csv	Total numbers, mean sizes, and percentage coverages of IBAs and AZEs in each GEO region	BirdLife International & AZE	http://dx.doi.org/10.5061/dryad.6gb90.2/7.2
IBAs_AZEs_IPBES.csv	Total numbers, mean sizes, and percentage coverages of IBAs and AZEs in each IPBES region and subregion		http://dx.doi.org/10.5061/dryad.6gb90.2/8.2
PAs_GEO.csv	Percentage protected area coverage of land and sea, for each GEO region and subregion	UNEP-WCMC & IUCN	http://dx.doi.org/10.5061/dryad.6gb90.2/9.2
PAs_IPBES.csv	Percentage protected area coverage of land and sea, for each IPBES region and subregion		http://dx.doi.org/10.5061/dryad.6gb90.2/10.2
Protected_IBAs_GEO.csv	Percentage of IBAs wholly covered by protected areas, over time, for each GEO region and subregion	BirdLife International, IUCN & UNEP-WCMC	http://dx.doi.org/10.5061/dryad.6gb90.2/11.2
Protected_IBAs_IPBES.csv	Percentage of IBAs wholly covered by protected areas, over time, for each IPBES region and subregion		http://dx.doi.org/10.5061/dryad.6gb90.2/12.2
Protected_AZEs_GEO.csv	Percentage of AZE sites wholly covered by protected areas, over time, for each GEO region and subregion	AZE, BirdLife International, IUCN & UNEP-WCMC	http://dx.doi.org/10.5061/dryad.6gb90.2/13.2
Protected_AZEs_IPBES.csv	Percentage of AZE sites wholly covered by protected areas, over time, for each IPBES region and subregion		http://dx.doi.org/10.5061/dryad.6gb90.2/14.2

Figure 3. Choice of Individual datasets published for biodiversity assessment

The key messages about the state of biodiversity in Africa, and the pressures upon it, which have emerged from this assessment (The State of Biodiversity in Africa: A mid-term review of progress towards the Aichi Biodiversity Targets) are:

- Overall, biodiversity in Africa continues to decline, with ongoing losses of species and habitats.

- Ongoing loss of biodiversity in Africa is driven by a combination of human-induced factors.

- Africa's freshwater ecosystems and their biodiversity are especially threatened.

- Africa continues to experience deforestation and forest degradation.

- The negative impacts of climate change on species and ecosystems are intensifying the effects of all these pressures.

- Nonetheless the report identifies a number of important responses which have taken place since 2011.

- African countries are working collaboratively to address particular Aichi Biodiversity Targets.

- There is a growing portfolio of international support for African countries to achieve the Aichi Biodiversity Targets.

- African countries are using ecosystem service valuation and investment in REDD+ to achieve the Aichi Biodiversity Targets.

19

- Many African countries have already achieved their 17% terrestrial protected area targets, and many others are working towards this target on land, as well as on the 10% marine protected areas target on the sea.

- Africa is making increasing use of ecosystem based conservation and restoration of natural resources.

Why do we need new technologies for sustainable development and biodiversity conservation?

The European Space Agency has issued on the 29th July 2016 an invitation to tender for the **GlobDiversity** project. GlobDiversity will conduct a set of activities for the definition, specification, benchmarking, prototyping, validation, scaling up and utility demonstration of High Resolution Remotely-Sensed Essential Biodiversity Variables (RS-EBVs) on the structure and function of terrestrial ecosystems, in support to the collaborative efforts of the CBD, IPBES and GEO BON to build a comprehensive and global knowledge of the state of and changes to the biological diversity of terrestrial ecosystems and the services they provide to society. EBVs are the abbreviation for Essential Biodiversity Variables. These Essential Biodiversity Variables, defined as the derived measurements required to study, report, and manage biodiversity change, focusing on status and trend in elements of biodiversity should play the role of brokers between monitoring initiatives and decision makers. The primary source of Earth Observation satellite data shall come from High Resolution (HR) satellite missions (in the range of 10m to 30m spatial resolution) that have free and open data policies and long-term observation continuity (e.g. EO4SD: Earth Observation for Sustainable Development). Priority shall be given to the Sentinel 1 and Sentinel 2 missions of the European Copernicus Program and to the Landsat 8 satellite of the US National Land Imaging Programme, both part of sustainable Earth Observation programmes that will secure the continuous and systematic collection of high-resolution remote sensing data over entire Earth land masses beyond 2030. The EO4SD is an example of an ESA initiative to support the uptake of EO-derived information in sustainable development (http://eo4sd.esa.int/).

An important player for the future assessment of Earth's biodiversity is GEO BON (Group On Earth Observations Biodiversity Observation Network; https://geobon.org/). The Global Biodiversity Information Facility (GBIF) and more recently the Group on Earth Observations – Biodiversity Observation Network (GEO BON) launched in 2008 under the Group on Earth Observations (GEO) initiative have been instrumental in stimulating the first global coordinated efforts to harmonise biodiversity observations and to better link in-situ and remotely-sensed information.

Take Home messages

There is a …

- Need for multi-disciplinary and multi-national group of researchers who have the endorsement of the international research community (e.g. UNEP, IPBES, Goettingen International Health Network, EuroLife)

- "Status Quo": Lack of integrated Data Bases for Environment research!

- Need for baseline data to be able to carry out investigations at the appropriate geographical scale and temporal scale!

- Urgent need for EO and GIS! Data, methods and education

- Assessment of pathways for mitigation / adaptation strategies

- Need for Modelling, Simulation, Risk and Vulnerability Assessment

- The use of geographic information system (GIS) is becoming increasingly widespread in research linking global change, health and the environment (linking also the different disciplines).

- Need for translation methods which take the language of science and turn them into the language of policy and action (without diminishing the importance of the science).

References

IPBES, 2018. Summary for policymakers of the regional assessment report on biodiversity and ecosystem services for Africa of the Intergovernmental Science-Policy Platform on Biodiversity and Ecosystem Services. E. Archer, L. E. Dziba, K. J. Mulongoy, M.

A. Maoela, M. Walters, R. Biggs, M-C. Cormier-Salem, F. DeClerck, M. C. Diaw, A. E. Dunham, P. Failler, C. Gordon, K. A. Harhash, R. Kasisi, F. Kizito, W. D. Nyingi, N. Oguge, B. Osman-Elasha, L. C. Stringer, L. Tito de Morais, A. Assogbadjo, B. N. Egoh, M. W. Halmy, K. Heubach, A. Mensah, L. Pereira and N. Sitas (eds.). IPBES secretariat, Bonn, Germany. 49 pages. https://www.ipbes.net/assessment-reports/africa

UNEP-WCMC, 2016. The State of Biodiversity in Africa: A mid-term review of progress towards the Aichi Biodiversity Targets. UNEP-WCMC, Cambridge, UK.

Jetz W., Cavender-bares, J., Pavlick R. Schimel D., Davis, F.W.,Asner, G.P., Guralnick, R., Kattge, J., Latimer, A:M:, Schaepman, M:E., Schildhauer, M.P., Schneider, F.D., Schrodt, F. Stahl, U. and S.L. Ustin, 2016. Monitoring plant functional diversity from space. Nature Plants 2, Article number: 16024. https://doi.org/10.1038/nplants.2016.24

Climate-Smart Agricultural Production in the Congo Basin of Central Africa

ERNEST L. MOLUA[1], DENIS SONWA[2], YOUSSOUFA BELE[2]

[1]Department of Agricultural Economics and Agribusiness Faculty of Agriculture & Veterinary Medicine, University of Buea, Cameroon

E-mail: emolua@cidrcam.org / emolua@yahoo.com

[2]Center for International Forestry Research, Yaounde, Cameroon

Abstract

Agriculture through deforestation is an important threat to the Congo basin forest. The aim of this research is to provide empirical evidence on the impact of farm-level investments on climate-smart agricultural practices related to agroforestry, conservation agriculture, and soil and water management efforts on agricultural output and income generation in the Congo Basin. The data was collected from more than 600 farms in Cameroon, Central African Republic and Democratic Republic of Congo. A Conditional Logit model test for farmer's choice of agricultural system and a farmland value regression for each system show that farmers choose one of three agricultural systems to maximize farm profit mindful of current tenure regime and environmental conditions. The rights to access, withdraw, manage, exclude others from land and trees affect both the farmer's choice of system and the net revenue earned from the chosen system.

Key words: Climate-smart agriculture, land management, Congo Basin Forests

Introduction

Congo Basin's interconnected tropical forest holds 70 percent of the total plant cover in the African continent, with a 2.9 ha of forest area per capita compared to a global forest area per capita of 0.8 ha. About 70 million people inhabit this trans-boundary pool of natural resources, with about 60 percent of whom still live in rural areas (FAO 2005) and depend directly on forest ecosystem goods and services for household consumption, including food, fuelwood and medicinal plants. They also generate income from the trade of many forest goods, especially non-timber forest products. In addition to its environmental services such as watershed management, soil and biodiversity conservation and carbon sequestration, the Congo Basin forest has enormous carbon stocks which represent a carbon reserve of global significance for regulating greenhouse gas (GHG) emissions in the atmosphere. However, agriculture is an important threat to the Congo basin forest's wealth. The vulnerability of the basin is thus underscored in livelihoods highly dependent on climate-sensitive sectors like forests for household energy, agriculture, fisheries, food security, pastoral practices, water supply, herbs and tree barks. Climate change will reinforce this vulnerability (Campbell 2009; Bonan 2008; Canadell & Raupach 2008; Justice et al., 2001).

According to Justice et al. (2001) Congo Basin Forests (CBF), a major transboundary natural resource pool spanning approximately 200 million hectares is likely to be impacted by climate change. With the second largest contiguous tract of humid tropical forest in the world after the Amazon basin forest and is the largest in Africa covering almost 2 million sq. km, the forest extends to six countries namely Cameroon, the Republic of Congo, the Democratic Republic of Congo (DRC), the Central African Republic (CAR), Gabon and Equatorial Guinea; with about 65 million people living inside and at the margins of the Basin, depending on it directly for livelihood. Subsistence small-scale slash-and-burn shifting cultivation is the dominant economic activity and farm practice of the inhabitants (Sonwa et al. 2011; Bellassen & Glitz, 2008; Zhang et al. 2002).

The goal of this paper is to provide empirical evidence on the impact of farm-level investments on climate-smart agricultural practices in the Congo Basin. Climate-smart agricultural practices are hereby defined, according to the FAO (2009) as those which offer "triple wins" in the areas of food security, adaptation, and mitigation. Such practices include techniques for soil and water management, pest control, conservation of genetic resources, and combining crops, trees, livestock, fisheries, etc., into integrated production systems. The hypothesis is that tenure security to land and trees play a fundamental role in governing the patterns of investment in crop and farmland management, as well as in the profitability of farms that depend on those resources. The development of conserving technologies for agricultural land use, their adaptation to local environments, and the knowledge and diffusion elements for sustainable agriculture are very important components.

Methodology

Analytical framework: Microeconometric model

A microeconometric model may be employed and refined to study how farming systems respond to institutions and environmental conditions. We first examine how farmers under different tenure arrangements may choose their respective farming systems (see e.g. Markovitz, 1952). In line with the empirical framework of Seo (2010), we assume that farmers choose one of three agricultural systems to maximize farm profit mindful of current tenure regime and environmental conditions. Based on the combination of crops and livestock that a farmer holds, three agricultural systems

(j) are distinguished: a specialized mixed arable cropping system, a specialized integrated tree – arable crop system (agri-silviculture), and a mixed tree arable crop-livestock system (agrosilvopastoral). The prevailing tenure arrangement will therefore affect both the farmer's choice of system and the net revenue earned from the chosen system (Kelly *et al.*, 2005). The novelty of this approach, distinct from previous cross-sectional studies, is that we expect to quantify adoption behaviors explicitly and measure differential effects on various agricultural systems.

Assuming the net revenue (π) from farm system j and 1 is written as follows:

$$\pi_1 = X\beta_1 + u_1 \qquad (1)$$

$$\pi_j^* = Z\gamma_j + \eta_j, \quad j = 1, \ldots, J. \qquad (2)$$

where $E(u_1|X,Z) = 0$ and $var(u_1|X,Z) = \sigma^2$ (Dubin and McFadden 1984), and the error terms may capture such factors as measurement errors, omitted variables, and other unobserved factors. These terms are assumed to average to zero and have equal variance. The subscript j is a categorical variable indicating the choice amongst J systems (in our analysis J =1 a specialized mixed arable cropping system, J = 2 denotes an agri-silviculture system, and J = 3 indicates an agrosilvopastoral system). Vector Z represents the set of explanatory variables relevant for all the alternatives and vector X contains the determinants of the profit of the first alternative, i.e. specialization in crops only. We identify choice equations by two variables: slope of terrain and walking time to district capital (Fisher 1966; Johnston & Dinardo 1997), which are excluded in the second stage regressions. The regressors for this paper include environmental and socioeconomic variables such as tenure (land ownership), education, gender, distance to markets and country dummies.

Scope, nature and source of data

Economic data used in this study came from CIFOR's Congo Basin Adaptation and Mitigation Project (COBAM) dataset on rural farms. The dataset is based on household surveys collected from more than 600 farms across three countries for farming activities during the period from January 2011 to March 2012. The survey elicited information about infrastructure and distance to markets, ethnic composition and extent of in-migration, cropping and livestock activities, tree species composition, major tree planting projects, prices of agricultural and wood products, natural and man-made shocks such as floods or war, and a set of tenure variables including rights over land and trees across broad tenure categories. Probability samples were drawn from Cameroon, Republic of Central Africa and Democratic Republic of Congo. In each country, three or four regions were selected to cover a broad range of environmental and socioeconomic conditions. This paper uses cross section data on 12 regions/provinces and 40 divisions in Cameroon, Central African Republic and Democratic Republic of Congo to determine statistically the factors determining farm profits. The analysis is performed using the STATA statistical software.

Results & Discussion

The perception of climate change is significant in the Congo basin, and climate change adaptation relating to adjustments in human and natural systems in response to actual or expected climatic variation with a view to moderating harm or exploiting beneficial opportunities, is increasing employed. Some of these measures simultaneously cater for both adaptation and mitigation.

A wide range of measures are employed to reduce the impact of agriculture and the sectors' climate-change footprint. For crop agriculture, these include soil, plant and water management. Table 1 indicates the variety of measures employed in the sub-region. Soil management practices are essentially through composting manure and crop residues, or using legumes for natural nitrogen fixation. These are employed to conserve soil nutrient levels on the acknowledgment that the availability of nitrogen and other nutrients is essential to increase yields. Avoidance of tillage minimizes occurrence of net losses of carbon dioxide by microbial respiration and oxidation of the soil organic matter and builds soil structure and biopores through soil biota and roots. Maintenance of a mulch layer provides a substrate for soil-inhabiting microorganisms which helps to improve and maintain water and nutrients in the soil. This also contributes to net increase of soil organic matter – derived from carbon dioxide captured by photosynthesis in plants, whose residues above and below the surface are subsequently transformed and sequestered by soil biota.

Table 1: climate-smart agricultural techniques in some communities in the Congo Basin

Soil nutrient management	Crop plant management	Water management	Ecosystem management	Harvesting and supply Chain management
Artificial fertilization Organic fertilization Minimal mechanical soil disturbance (i.e. zero tillage, minimum tillage and direct seeding) Permanent soil cover	altering cropping patterns planting dates farm management techniques. new drought tolerant varieties diversifying production systems growing other cultivars mixed farming of cereals, vegetables and rearing animals (such as pigs and chickens).	Trash lines Stone bunds Log lines Water pits Stream irrigation	Surface residue retention, e.g. maintenance of a mulch of carbon-rich organic matter covering and feeding the soil (e.g. straw and/or other crop residues including cover crops); and rotations or sequences and associations (intercropping) of crops which could include nitrogen-fixing legumes. Tree planting and tree management	Improved storage Packaging Semi-processing Cooperatives (producer or marketing)
Notes: Farmers tend to employ more than one measure. Collated from Survey data, 2012				

Using methods and practices that increases organic nutrient inputs, retention and use are seen as fundamental and reduces the need of synthetic fertilizers which, due to cost and access, are often unavailable to smallholders. Management of soil fertility and organic matter, and improvement of the efficiency of nutrient inputs, enable more production with proportionally less fertilizers. It also saves on energy use in farming and reduces emissions from the burning of crop residues. Moreover it helps sequester carbon in soil. Crop plant management through spacing, weeding, pruning and thinning are geared towards effective vegetative growth and controlling pest and disease proliferation, in cognizant that climate variation and change are altering the distribution, incidence and intensity of animal and plant pests and diseases as well as invasive and alien species. These efforts are in tandem with water harvesting and retention through pools, dams, pits, retaining ridges, which are fundamental for increasing production and addressing enlarged irregularity of rainfall patterns.

Livestock producers employ measures which include improving production and feed systems, developing new breeds of ruminant, introducing methods of manure management which reduce emissions, and integrating livestock with crops (annual and perennials) in order to reduce waste and improve soil fertility. Improved grazing management, the efficient treatment of manure, and the substitution of manure for inorganic fertilizers are asserted to have the capacity to lower emissions and improve soil condition and productivity. The reintegration of livestock with crop activities, the strategic location of intensive livestock production units and enhanced processing techniques to reduce production losses are also effective strategies for boosting productivity. Mixed farming of cereals, vegetables and rearing animals (such as pigs and chickens), and the residues and waste from each system are being composted and used on the land, thereby reducing the need for external inputs. This diversification has increased incomes, improved nutrition, built resilience to shocks and minimized financial risks.

Ecosystem management through the adoption of different natural resource management and production practices is actively been promoted by public and private institutions. These are noted to include: surface residue retention, intercropping and farmland tree management provides for resilient, productive and sustainable systems which control pests and disease, regulate microclimate, decompose wastes, regulate nutrient cycles and crop pollination. Agroforestry, i.e. the use of trees and shrubs in agricultural crop and/or animal production and land management systems is the dominant practice, given the attraction of the product and service function of trees. For instance, trees can improve soil fertility and soil moisture through increasing soil organic matter. Nitrogen-fixing leguminous trees and shrubs can be especially important to soil fertility where there is limited access to mineral fertilizers. Improved soil fertility tends to increase agricultural productivity and may allow more flexibility in the types of crops that can be grown. Agroforestry systems are important sources of timber and fuelwood. These systems tend to sequester much greater quantities of carbon than agricultural systems without trees. Planting trees in agricultural lands is relatively efficient and cost effective compared to other mitigation strategies, and provides a range of co-benefits important for improved farm family livelihoods and climate change adaptation.

Table 2. Farm revenue regressions conditional on agricultural systems (FCFA/ha)

Variables	Arable crops	Agri-silviculture	Agrosilvopastoral
Area exploited (ha)	1.34**	1.73	2.49
	(1.64)	(1.55)	1.73)
Age, household head	6.09	4.32	9.35
(years)	(4.13)	(2.12)	(5.31)
Gender, household head	5.92	7.23	3.94
	(3.13)	(4.40)	(1.58)
Schooling, household	6.46	9.16	11.32
head (years)	(2.11)	(5.17)	(7.21)
Family size	4.39**	5.51*	2.72
	(1.62)	(2.15)	(1.19)
Nativity	1.25	1.33	2.96
	(2.38)	(7.29)	(9.38)
Walking time to plot	-3.75	-9.93	-12.61
	(3.26)	(4.25)	(45.31)
Joint family	1.47	1.36	1.97**
	(1.48)	(2.46)	(2.95)
Single family	1.47	1.58*	1.86
	(4.19)	(5.52)	(6.43)
Private ownership	2.89**	2.47	2.93
(Purchase)	(1.82)	(1.25)	(1.78)
Clearance	1.39**	1.86	1.29*
	(1.21)	(1.70)	(1.08)
Credit	230.25	125.83	623.32**
	(22.38)	(35.48)	(40.36)
Soil management	3.43*	3.85	4.68
	(7.59)	(5.17)	(9.83)
Crop management	2.97*	2.65*	2.73
	(2.92)	(1.64)	(1.35)
Water management	2.81*	4.76	5.99**
	(1.76)	(1.81)	(1.09)
Ecosystem management	3.12*	6.96*	8.79*
	(5.32)	(4.93)	(3.18)
Supply chain	15.51	23.48	19.19
management	(5.05)	(3.004)	(8.001)
Access to climate	2.17	5.23	7.96
information	(0.99)	(0.08)	(0.09)
Age, household head	6.09	4.32	9.35
(years)	(4.13)	(2.12)	(5.31)
Gender, household head	5.92	7.23	3.94
	(3.13)	(4.40)	(1.58)
Schooling, household	6.46	9.16	11.32
head (years)	(2.11)	(5.17)	(7.21)

Family size	4.39**	5.51*	2.72
	(1.62)	(2.15)	(1.19)
Nativity	1.25	1.33	2.96
	(2.38)	(7.29)	(9.38)
Walking time to plot	-3.75	-9.93	-12.61
	(3.26)	(4.25)	(45.31)
Joint family	1.47	1.36	1.97**
	(1.48)	(2.46)	(2.95)
Single family	1.47	1.58*	1.86
	(4.19)	(5.52)	(6.43)
Private ownership (Purchase)	2.89**	2.47	2.93
	(1.82)	(1.25)	(1.78)
Clearance	1.39**	1.86	1.29*
	(1.21)	(1.70)	(1.08)
Credit	230.25	125.83	623.32**
	(22.38)	(35.48)	(40.36)
Soil management	3.43*	3.85	4.68
	(7.59)	(5.17)	(9.83)
Crop management	2.97*	2.65*	2.73
	(2.92)	(1.64)	(1.35)
Water management	2.81*	4.76	5.99**
	(1.76)	(1.81)	(1.09)
Ecosystem management	3.12*	6.96*	8.79*
	(5.32)	(4.93)	(3.18)
Supply chain management	15.51	23.48	19.19
	(5.05)	(3.004)	(8.001)
Access to climate information	2.17	5.23	7.96
	(0.99)	(0.08)	(0.09)
Access to extension services	3.22	8.68	12.27**
	(0.35)	(0.68)	(0.36)
RCA	78.63	75.68	89.77*
	(7.74)	(8.82)	(9.93)
DRC	124.82	133.69	270.97*
	(8.18)	(5.67)	(6.90)
Intercept	13500.19	24810.58	35700.33
	(5.13)	(9.54)	(5.83)
Number of observations	256	196	148
Log likelihood	-367.64	-317.82	-261.56

Notes: (1) The omitted choice is integrated crop-specialized livestock system. (2) For the country dummy, Cameroon is treated as the base case. (3)The goodness of fit measures: McFadden's LRI = 0.13, Veall-Zimmermann = 0.27. (4) P-value of the Likelihood Ratio test of the set of tenure variables: < 0.0001. (5). Numbers in parentheses are Heteroscedasty Consistent Standard Errors. * indicates significance at 10% while ** at 5%. Computed from Survey Data, 2012

Improving farm income and producer welfare is a *sine qua non* in stimulating the adoption and use of modern farm practices. Moreover the acknowledgment that production is not complete until the goods reach the final consumer, harvesting and supply chain management are employed with improved storage, better packaging, semi-processing and participation in farmer cooperatives (whether producer and/or marketing). The goal is on efficient harvesting and early transformation of agricultural production to reduce post-harvest losses and preserve the quantity, quality and nutritional value of the product. Information dissemination through farmer field school programmes in Cameroon encourages better use of co-products and by-products, either as feed for livestock, to produce renewable energy in integrated systems or to improve soil fertility. However, where supply chains become longer and more complex, challenges related to operational efficiency of processing, packaging, storage and transport become very important. Overall, however, the plethora of measures imply that there is no blueprint for climate-smart agriculture, and its precise nature will vary from place to place, influenced by a whole host of local factors, including the climate, the crops grown, the livestock reared, available technologies and the knowledge and skills of individual farmers.

We run regressions of farm returns (gross revenue) against tenure and other control variables for each system (Table 2). Tenure has differential effects. For example, cleared forest and single family owned farms increase the value of the crop-only system and the mixed system, but decrease that of the arable crop-only system because of the higher investments required for the more complex farming system. When a family is large and household head is older, the farmland used for the crop-only system experiences higher returns. When the farm-head has more years of schooling, the revenue from mixed farming system is observed to increase. Ecosystem management significantly contributes to revenue in all three systems more than the other management practices, perhaps due to the marketable wood and non-wood products from tree crops in farmlands. However, crop and water management as climate-smart practices are lowly significant in crop-only systems. Water management is more significant in integrated crop-tree-livestock systems. The country dummies are also significant. The gross revenue for the tree-crop-livestock is lower in RCA than in Cameroon, which is the base case. The revenue for the three systems is significantly higher in DRC.[1]

---

[1] Two measures of the goodness of fit, given under the table, are high, ranging from 0.12 (McFadden's LRI) to 0.27 (Veall-Zimmermann). The tenure variables as a whole are highly significant determinants

Conclusion

This paper examined whether an integrated farming system which manages crops, trees and livestock would be selected than the more profitable specialized farms when faced with tenure constraints. We developed a micro-econometric selection model which explains both changes in choices and net revenues simultaneously. The results establish that whether de jure ownership or secure long-term rights of access to land, particularly in the form of locally recognized use rights, create an incentive for people to make farmland-improving investments such as water harvesting or other investments in soil erosion control; and whether insecure or short-term rights of access may have an opposite effect. The model which endogenizes perception of climate change, indicate that current choices and land values of agricultural systems across the Congo Basin are sensitive to land rights. It also indicates that integrated farming technique may be chosen most often when the existing tenure arrangements provide for ownership rights, and less so when under mere user rights in extended family joint ownership. When the tenure constraints are eased, farmers switch from arable crops to tree crops and livestock integrated multiple farming.

References

CGIAR, 2012. CGIAR research programs on Collective Action and Property Rights (CAPRi) and Climate Change, Agriculture and Food Security (CCAFS), Washington DC.

Dubin, Jeffrey A., and Daniel L. McFadden, 1984. An Econometric Analysis of Residential Electric Appliance Holdings and Consumption. Econometrica 52: 345–362.

FAO, 2011. The State of Forests in the Amazon Basin, Congo Basin and Southeast Asia. A report prepared for the Summit of the Three Rainforest Basins, Brazzaville, Republic of Congo, 31 May–3 June, 2011. Food and Agricultural Organisation of the United Nations

FAO, 2009. Enabling Agriculture to contribute to climate change mitigation. http://unfccc.int/resource/docs/2008/smsn/igo/036.pdf

FAO, 2009. Food security and agricultural mitigation in developing countries: Options for Capturing Synergies. ftp://ftp.fao.org/docrep/fao/012/ak596e/ak596e00.pdf

Fisher & M. Franklin, 1966. The Identification Problem in Econometrics. New York, McGraw-Hill.

of the agricultural system according to the P-value of the Likelihood Ratio test. From the estimated parameters, the model predicts a current agricultural system accurately for 61% of the entire sample. The predictive power of the model falls to 45%, however, when tenure variables are dropped from the model. The Adjusted R-sq is 0.26 for the crop-only system, 0.38 for the crop-tree only system, and 0.53 for the mixed system. As the land value of a specific agricultural system is observed only when the system is chosen, we correct for selection biases from the farmlands that are used for the other systems).

Johnston, J. & J. Dinardo, 1997. Econometric Methods 4th ed. New York, McGraw-Hill.

Kelly, D.L., C.D. Kolstad, & G.T. Mitchell, 2005. Adjustment Costs from Environmental Change", *Journal of Environmental Economics and Management* 50: 468–495.

Kurukulasuriya, Pradeep, et al., 2006. "Will African Agriculture Survive Climate Change?" *World Bank Economic Review* 20: 367–388.

Markovitz, H., 1952, Portfolio Selection. *Journal of Finance* 7:77–91.

McFadden & L. Daniel, 1974. Conditional Logit Analysis of Qualitative Choice Behavior. In: Frontiers in Econometrics, ed. P. Zarembka, 105–142. New York: Academic Press.

McFadden, D.L. & K. Train, 2000. Mixed MNL Models for Discrete Response", *Journal of Applied Econometrics* 15: 447–470.

How Policy Change Happens: Incorporating the SDGs into the SADA Master Plan to further Localization and Harmonization of SDGs in the Northern Savannah Ecological Zone (NSEZ) of Ghana

JOSEPH ABAZAAMI

Institute for Interdisciplinary Research and Consultancy Services
University for Development Studies
Post Office Box TL 1350, Tamale, Ghana

Email: abazaami@yahoo.com

Abstract

As part of the implementation of Agenda 2030, the Government of Ghana, through the National Development Planning Commission (NDPC), made it a priority that the Sustainable Development Goals (SDGs) be integrated into all levels of development planning: national, sub-national and decentralized administrative levels. In this context, it became imperative that the Savannah Accelerated Development Authority (SADA), which was mandated by Act 805 (2010) to fast track the long term and comprehensive economic and social transformation of the Northern Savannah Ecological Zone (NSEZ), took the necessary steps to ensure that its sub-national planning processes, notably the SADA Master Plan, properly incorporated and reflected the SDGs.This paper explores the efforts the author made to facilitate the successful integration of the SDGs into the SADA Master Plan. It highlights the identification and prioritization of indicators that were contextually relevant to the NSEZ; the availability (or otherwise) of quality, timely and relevant data at the sub-national level; the identification of data gaps, and the exploration of innovative methods for resolving the identified data issues.

Background

Located in West Africa, Ghana is bordered by the Gulf of Guinea and Atlantic Ocean to the south, Cote d'Ivoire to the west, Burkina Faso to the north and Togo to the east. The Northern Savannah Ecological Zone (NSEZ) covers approximately 54% of the country's total land area in Northern Ghana and has an existing population of 5.3 million (SADA, 2016). The key issues facing the NSEZ include an agriculture dependent economy; unemployment and low productivity; low literacy and low levels of social facilities; lack of a developed and integrated transport and infrastructure; as well as the threat of environmental degradation. However, the NSEZ possesses significant comparative advantages and has tremendous untapped potential – it has about six million hectares of arable land with great potential for commercial production of cereals, sugarcane, cassava, cotton, cashew, shea and livestock (World Bank, 2017).

As part of the implementation of Agenda 2030, the Government of Ghana (GoG), through the National Development Planning Commission (NDPC), made it a priority that the Sustainable Development Goals (SDGs) be integrated at all levels of development planning (national, sub-national and decentralized) administrative levels. In this context, it became imperative that the Savannah Accelerated Development Authority (SADA, renamed, Northern Development Authority-NADA in 2017), which was mandated by the SADA Act 805 (2010) *"to fast track the long term and comprehensive economic and social transformation of the Northern Savannah Ecological Zone"* (NSEZ), took the necessary steps to ensure that its sub-national planning processes, notably the SADA Master Plan, properly incorporated and reflected the SDGs.

This was in the light of policy developments as in the following spheres:

a) At the global level, there had been transformational change with the translation of the MDGs to SDGs,

b) Within the context of Africa, Agenda 2063 is seeking to shift Africa into an accelerated gear of development informed by economic strengthening with culture being a cornerstone to the process,

c) In the context of Ghana, there were frantic efforts to complete the preparation of a 40 year Long Term National Development Plan (LTNDP) seeking to guide the nation's journey towards a just, free and prosperous society; and last but not least,

d) The peculiar nuances explicit between the ten Ghana Shared Growth and Development Agenda II and the SADA Master Plan

These policy developments called for the need to reconcile SADA's Master Plan's goals, objectives, targets and indicators with those spelt out under the SDGs, Agenda 2063 and Ghana's LTNDP in order to comprehensively be in sync with developments at the global, regional and national levels. In view of the fact that these policy developments were binding on Ghana and for that matter of SADA (NSEZ), there was an urgent need to develop capacity to track results and to use that knowledge to learn what does and what does not work or how to make things work better.

The process leading to the adoption of SDGs in the context of SADA's Master Plan had been all inclusive. Data requirements for monitoring the 17 SDGs and 169 targets, the 7 Aspirations and the 20 derived goals of Agenda 2063 placed great responsibility on all data producers and users in Ghana and the NSEZ. The need to harness all resources and work together to identify data availability, frequency of data production, and levels of data disaggregation became very imperative in the process of ensuring that SADA's M&E framework was robust enough to measure sustainable development outcomes in the NSEZ.

SADA Regional Concept and Master Plan

The Government of Ghana (GoG) in 2010 through the SADA Act (805) set in motion an ambitious programme aimed at transforming the Northern part of Ghana economically and socially. The Act mandates SADA to provide the framework for the comprehensive and long term development of the NSEZ and provide for related matters. Key objectives of SADA comprise:

− Provinding strategic planning guidance to government for the zone

− Mobilizing resources to implement accelerated development

− Coordinating existing and future development policies affecting the zone for coherence.

To advance the objectives under its mandate, SADA launched a progressive initiative in 2015 to prepare a Regional Master Plan for the NSEZ comprising 5 Regions: Northern, Upper East and West, Brong Ahafo and Volta regions. The Plan details the following: Vision and Strategy Framework; Regional Structure Plan of SADA Zone; City Master Plan and regulatory framework for Tamale and Buipe; Urban Design for core areas of Tamale and Buipe; Implementation Plan and game changer's projects; City Gallery; Master Plan on-line; and Land Management System.

Surbana Jurong (consultants from Singapore) working closely with and through a number of Ghanaian professionals (including the Author) and stakeholders comprising the Town and Country Planning Department (TCPD), National Development Planning Commission (NDPC), professional commissions, UN agencies and local authorities set out to prepare the plan. Having progressively reached the final task of preparing the Regional Concept Plan, after the completion of the initial activities including data inventory, GIS database creation, context analysis, as well as socio-economic study to assess the dimensions of growth and identify potentials in NSEZ, it became apparent in 2016 that an important step was missed with the coming into being of the SDGs – as the Master Plan did not sufficiently cover all relevant goals, targets and indicators of Agenda 2030.

Given Ghana's decision to incorporate the SDGs into all national plans and the fact that most of the Goals of Agenda 2063 are aligned with the SDGs, SADA in partnership with Ghana Statistical Service (GSS) and relevant stakeholders initiated a process in 2016 to review the global set of SDG indicators to determine those that can be monitored by the National Statistical System (NSS) and how these could find expression in the SADA Master Plan. The review generally focused on: data availability for each indicator (classified as tier I, II or III[1]); data sources; institutions producing the data; most recent year data availability; frequency of compilation; levels of disaggregation; other possible data sources etc. This paper lays bare the availability (or otherwise) of quality, timely and relevant data at the sub-national (NSEZ) level, the identification of data gaps, and the exploration of innovative methods for resolving identified data issues to facilitate the process of making the SADA Master Plan SDG-compliant.

Study Process and Methodology

The first stage of the exercise was a comprehensive systematic review of literature, activities and empirical studies that informed the regional concept and master planning process. The figure 1 presents a schematic view of the steps of the process.

For each of the steps, efforts were made to appreciate relevant goals, targets and indicators in agenda 2030 that were missing and needed redress by way of incorporation into the regional concept and master plan. Similarly, the extent to which the regional concept and master plan was vertically and horizontally aligned to Agenda 2030 was explored by delving deeply into the Ghana Spatial Development Framework; NSEZ Spatial Development Framework; National Sectoral Plans, policies and standards; other existing local and regional plans and policies etc. The rationale was to ensure that SADA's regional concept and master plan was not at variance with these existing frameworks, plans and policies in the quest to be in sync with Agenda 2030.

---

[1] Tier I: Indicator conceptually clear, established methodology and standards available, data regularly produced by countries. Tier II: Indicator conceptually clear, established methodology and standards available, but data not regularly produced by countries. Tier III: Indicator for which an internationally agreed methodology has not yet been developed.

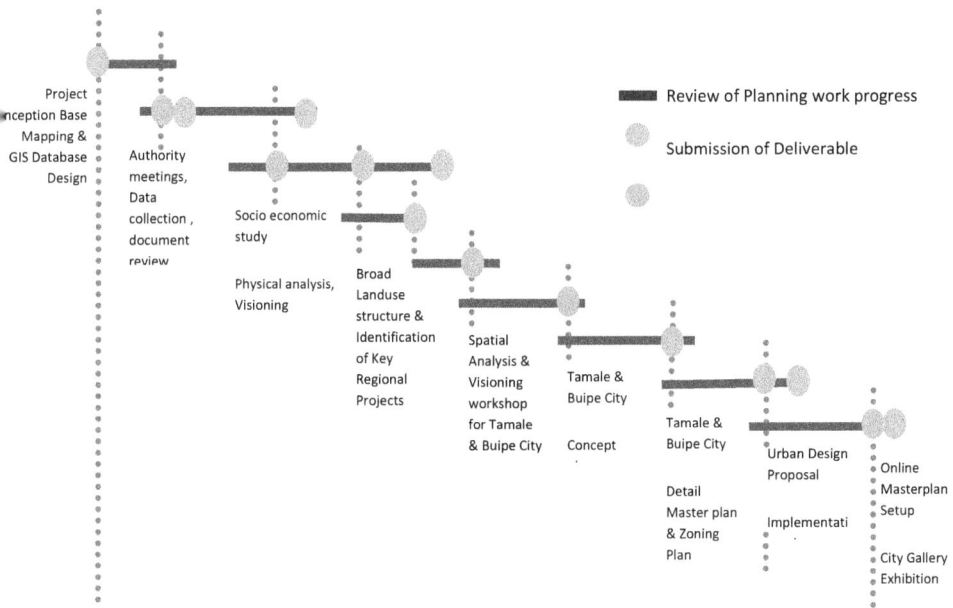

Figure 1. Systematic Review of Planning Process and Timelines

The second significant stage of the process was the constructive and interactive stakeholders' and focus group meetings which sought to gather valuable inputs to guide the harmonization of the Regional Concept Plan with Agenda 2030. This included meetings and discussions with the Steering Committee, Technical Committee as well as the Regional Oversight Team, which comprised stakeholders from multiple disciplines and institutions, along with representatives from the 5 respective regions of NSEZ.

These technical engagements furthered the SDGs localization agenda in the SADA zone by ensuring (1) that the SDGs were properly reflected in the SADA regional concept and master plan; and (2) that the SDGs that stakeholders prioritize in the SADA zone are relevant and meaningful at the local level. Moreover, these engagements additionally served the objective of helping to identify SDG targets and indicators that were relevant to decentralized planning and how these could be to aligned to the SADA Zone master planning ambitions. These constructive engagements also provided the framework for the discussion (and exploration) of data availability, data gaps for baseline and routine monitoring, as well various ways of

39

generating requisite data for sub-national planning, monitoring and evaluation of the SDGs in the SADA Zone.

Results and Findings

Outcome of Data Review

Juxtaposing the goals, objectives and aspirations of the SADA Regional Concept Plan as summarized in figure 2 above to the 17 interlinked SDGs, 169 targets and 230 plus indicators of Agenda 2030, the following realities became explicit:

- 56 indicators were found to have already been compiled by the Ghana National Statistical System (NSS) – 27 of these indicators were from administrative data sources;

- 57 indicators were not yet compiled by the National Statistical System but data existed for their computation – 36 of these indicators were from administrative data sources; and

- 113 of the global indicators (tier I & II) were either compiled within the National Statistical System or data existed for their computation – 63 of these indicators were identified to be in the process of being compiled through administrative data sources.

Following from this review, it became worthwhile for SADA to collaborate more closely with the Ghana Statistical Service (GSS) and other related institutions to address the data gaps identified. Indeed the GSS used the process to identify indicators that could be monitored in their current survey programme (i.e. Round 7 of the Ghana Living Standards Survey – GLSS 7). GLSS 7 among other interests was billed to collect data for monitoring 36 of the 113 indicators.

It is apparent from the foregoing that, the GSS needs to improve strategies for increasing statistics production by forging new partnerships for increased access to timely, relevant and conceptually sound data to advance the accurate monitoring and evaluation of the SDGs not only within the context of SADA's Master Plan but the nation as a whole. Similarly, the data gaps identified clearly pointed to the need for the GSS to explore new forms of social and geophysical data and innovative means of data collection and sharing to improve the tracking of the SDGs in Ghana.

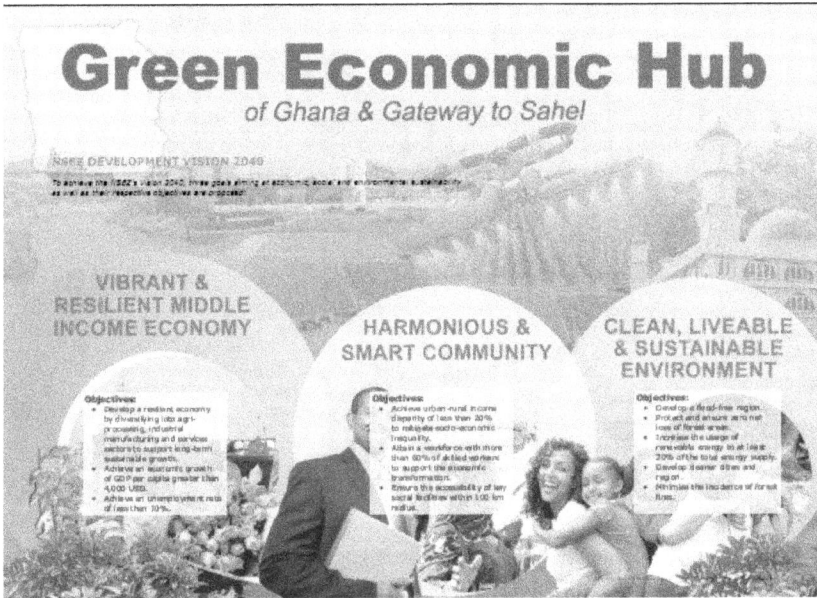

Figure 2. Summary of the Regional Concept and Master Plan

Source: SADA. 2016. Regional Concept Plan of the NSEZ. Draft Version.

Outcome of Stakeholder Engagements

Within a workshop setting, multi and interdisciplinary teams of experts (3 Expert Groups) were constituted to carry out in-depth assessment and mapping of the SADA Goals and objectives to the SDGs and targets. The mapping exercises of the Expert Groups were harmonized to identify points of convergence and divergence with the view to reaching consensus on thorny issues of disagreement to chart the way forward in terms of constructive academic and practical understanding. The outcome of this exercise is summarized in Table 1 below:

Table 1. Summary of SADA Stakeholders' Review of SDGs and Master Plan

SADA Goals	SADA Objectives	Relevant SDG Goals and Targets
Thriving resilient middle income economy	Achieving GDP per capita of >US$ 5000; developing resilient and diversified economy; and ensuring unemployment rate of <10%	Goal 1: Targets 1 to 7 Goal 2: Targets 1 to 8 Goal 7: Targets 1 to 5 Goal 8: Targets 1 to 12
Harmonious and smart community	achieving urban-rural income disparity of < 20%; Attaining >60% of workforce as skilled workers; Ensuring key social facilities are accessible within 100 km radius.	Goal 4: Targets 1 to 10 Goal 10: Targets 1 to 10 Goal 16: Targets 1 to 12 Goal 9: Targets 1 to 8 Goal 3: Targets 1 to 13 Goal 5: Targets 1 to 9
Sustainable, clean and liveable environment	Developing a flood free region; Ensuring zero net loss of forest areas; Increasing use of renewable energy supply; and Developing cleaner cities and region	Goal 11: Targets 1 to 10 Goal 13: Targets 1 to 6 Goal 15: Targets 1 to 12 Goal 17: Targets 1 to 19 Goal 12: Targets 1 to 11 Goal 6: Targets 1 to 8

Source: SADA, 2016.

The salient findings are as follows:

- All the SDGs in the exception of Goal 14 (**Conserve and sustainably use the oceans, seas, and marine resources**) were found to be relevant in the light of the goals and aspirations of the SADA Regional Concept and Master Plan. SDG 14 was particularly found to be an outlier in view of the location of the NSEZ – not only is it far from being contiguous with the coast or marine resources, its interaction with these areas is at best very remote;

- SDGs 1, 2, 7&8 were found to be more closely in sync with the Regional Concept and Master Plan's goal of a **"thriving resilient middle income economy"** with all targets under these goals completely in line and spot on;

- SDGs 3, 4, 5, 10, 13&16 were found to be closely knit to the Regional Concept and Master Plan's goal of a **"harmonious and smart community"** with most targets having stronger affinity to this thematic area. It was established that while SDG 10 **(Reduce inequality within and among countries)** was very relevant to this goal, important targets under this theme such as targets 5, 6, 8&10 were not provided for in the plan. This became an important niche that needed to be filled in our quest to update and harmonize the plan with relevant indicators from Agenda 2030.

- SDGs 6, 11, 12, 13, 15&17 turned out to be strongly aligned to the plan's goal of a **"sustainable, clean and liveable environment"** however; goals 12 and 17 had very important and relevant targets that were not given expression in the plan. In respect of SDG 12 **(Ensure sustainable consumption and production patterns)** provision was not made for targets 1&11. A good chunk of the targets under SDG 17 **(Revitalize the global partnership for sustainable development)** was not provided for in the plan and this was for a good cause. It was observed that although targets 2,4,10–13 and 15 where important to the NSEZ, they were frame conditions expected to be facilitated from the developed world through the UN system and so presented little choice variables for planning within the frame of SADA's Regional Concept and Master Plan.

By way of summary of emerging issues, it would be worthwhile to acknowledge that the SDGs are not exclusively aligned to specific goals of SADA's Regional Concept and Master Plan but do have reinforcing and co-benefits with other goals. What is significant and apparent is that some of the SDGs are more aligned to some SADA goals than others and for planning purposes; this needed to be made explicit.

Conclusion

The 2030 Agenda for SD speaks to a certain way of working and SADA as a matter of course must have a firm appreciation of this in order to put in place the required capacity to monitor indicators that reliably reflect results at all stages of the development process – from strategic planning to implementation to completion. Developing a M&E system that tracks indicators using accurate and timely data is a natural priority for the SADA Zone. For agencies and institutions involved in SADA's transformational agenda, this means developing a common framework that will enable government and donor agencies to harmonize their monitoring activities. What in effect has been achieved through this exercise is a move towards defining a strategy for developing NSEZ M&E capacity as part of the overall SADA strategy and being in sync with the SDGs

In sum, the outcome of this exercise was the ability to place SADA in a position to be able to:

- Identify and prioritize sustainable development goals, targets and indicators that are relevant and meaningful to stakeholders in the NSEZ as well as tease out indicators for measuring the ambitious and transformational goals in the SADA Master Plan.

- Identify data challenges and gaps at the sub-national level and provide recommendations for meeting those challenges to enhance the acquisition and production of needed data for the effective tracking, monitoring and evaluation of the SDGs in the SADA Zone.

- Align the prioritized SDGs with the transformational goals of the SADA Master Plan.

References

SADA, 2016. Regional Concept Plan of the Northern Savannah Ecological Zone. *Concept Master Plan Report.* Draft Version: July 2016.

United Nations, 2015. *Transforming Our World: The 2030 Agenda for Sustainable Development.* New York: UN Publishing.

World Bank, 2017. Ghana: Agricultural Sector Policy Note. Transforming Agriculture for Economic Growth, Job Creation and Food Security. Agriculture Global Practice

AFR01, June, 2017. documents.worldbank.org/curated/en/336541505459269020/pdf/119753-PN-P133833-PUBLIC-Ghana-Policy-Note-Ag-Sector-Review.pdf (accessed 15.12.2018).

Quantifying soil organic carbon under contrasting land uses in Ethiopia: A review

CHUKWUEBUKA C. OKOLO*, GIRMAY GEBRESAMUEL, ABEBA N. RETTA, AMANUEL ZENEBE AND MITIKU HAILE

Department of Land Resources Management and Environmental Protection, Mekelle University, P.O. Box 231, Mekelle, Ethiopia

*Email of corresponding author: okolochukwuebuka@gmail.com

Abstract

In the face of climate change and global warming, scientists globally are striving for effective techniques on how best to sequester carbon in order to reduce global warming and achieve environmental sustainability. This paper reviews the available literature on the influence of various land use changes on gains and/or losses of soil carbon (C) stocks in Ethiopia. Irrespective of soil type, C stocks in the top soil (0–30 cm) were found to be higher than at sub-soil depths. Even though there is significant improvement in C sequestration in exclosures and community forests, the level of C sequestered is still below that of church forests. Conversion of native forest to other land uses resulted in a significant decrease in the SOC stocks across Ethiopia. Absence of long-term field trials and non-existence of SOC database are among the major drawbacks of SOC studies in Ethiopia identified in this review. With better management practices, it is possible to restore depleted C stocks even in degraded lands and to conserve C in more pristine lands across the rugged landscapes of Ethiopia.

Keywords: Agroecosystem, Climate change, Carbon sequestration, Land degradation, Luvisols, Resilience, Vertisols

Introduction

Rapid deforestation and degradation of forest resources that remains a major problem in Ethiopia is affecting the climate change (for example increase in average temperature, and variability in rainfall pattern). According to the World Bank (2010), Ethiopia remains one of the countries most vulnerable to climate change. More so, the rugged landscapes of Ethiopia, especially northern Ethiopia have witnessed unprecedented degradation occasioned by agricultural intensification and land misuse for the past three millennia (Nyssen et al. 2015). Different land uses and soil management practices have variable contributions towards the nature, quality and quantity of carbon (C) storage and/or CO_2 emission. The potential of soil to sequester carbon cannot be over-emphasized, and with approximately 2344 gigatone (Gt) (1 gigatone = 1 billion tones) of global organic carbon storage (Lal, 2004), making soil the largest terrestrial pool of organic carbon (Stockmann *et al.* 2013).

This review intends to summarize and synthesize available literatures (past and present research findings) on soil carbon sequestration (viz-a-viz C concentration and stock) in the tropics with special focus on Ethiopia. Findings of this review will form the integral basis for improved policy formulation and concerted efforts towards ensuring sustainable land use and C storage across different landscapes in tropical agroecosystems.

Methodology

For the purpose of this review, we reported both soil organic C concentration and stock to represent soil organic carbon (SOC) pool. The methodological approach adopted was literature search, which was carried out using the following search engines and platforms: Web of Science (apps.webofknowledge.com), Research Gate (https://www.researchgate .net), Google Scholar (scholar.google.com), AGRIS (agris.fao.org), and Science Direct (www.sciencedireect.com). Related PhD and MSc theses and dissertations (unpublished) sourced from different university archives were also used for this review. Literatures published up to 2018 were used as the benchmark, while "soil carbon sequestration under different land uses and climate change mitigation" were uses as key words. Our emphasis was only on SOC studies, thus articles on soil inorganic carbon (SIC) were not included in this review. The major land uses reported in the literature include: natural forest, agroforestry, church forest, controlled grazing, open communal grazing, rainfed crop production, irrigation based crop production, agroforestry, silvopasture, irrigation based fruit production, exclosure and grassland. Analytical methods used in all the reported studies varies, and included wet (Walkley and Black) and dry (dichromate) combustion method, Isotope ratio mass spectrometer, Infra-red spectroscopy and reflectance spectrometer for SOC determination.

Uncertainties in soil organic carbon studies

Contrast to previous researchers, Powlson *et al.* (2011) and Stockmann *et al.*(2013) argued that increased levels of SOC with the adoption different approaches and management practices does not literally translate to capture or allocation of extra C from the atmosphere to land. However, this might just be due to ordinary movement of C within the biosphere from one pool to another, without any negative or positive consequences for climate change. This implies that not all findings reporting increased SOC in land uses under different management practices are actually C capture from the atmosphere. Powlson et al. (2008) further recommended the term 'accumulation' to represent increases in SOC while 'sequestration' should be specifically used for scenarios and circumstances of significant extra transfer or capture of C from the atmosphere, which represents a valid approach to mitigating climate change. Therefore, this assertion needs to be critically examined by researchers in view of providing a clear mechanistic understanding of SOC sequestration and dynamics in the face of climate change. Site-specific conditions, soil types and dynamic nature of environmental dependent variables (pH, temperature, precipitation, and various anthropogenic activities) were potential sources of variations in the reported SOC pool. More so, differences in analytical methods employed by the researchers may have accounted for the variations in the trend of C pool reported in this review.

Previous scientific evidence of soil organic carbon distribution in Ethiopia

Ethiopia is strategically located in the horn of Africa (2°54'N-15°18' N latitude and 32°42'E – 48°18' E longitude). A land-locked country with massive land area of 1.12 million km^2 (Shiferaw et al. 2013), coupled with diverse climate, parent material, land use, geology and topography giving rise to a wide heterogeneity of soil types (Hurni et al. 2007; Mesfin 1998; Haileslassie 2005). According to the FAO (1986) as reported in Haileslassie et al. (2005), soils of Ethiopia are mainly of volcanic origin and Lithosols (14.7%), Nitosols (13.5%), Cambisols (11.1%), Regosols (12%) and Vertisols (10.5%) proportionally cover the country's vast area of landmass.

Most of the SOC researches were conducted in the southern part of Ethiopia, thus not giving a comprehensive clear overview of the trend in total soil carbon distribution data across different landscapes and regions of Ethiopia, which this review intends to address systematically. For example in the highlands of southern Ethiopia, changes in SOC stock was investigated by Lemenih et al. (2005) after reforestation of previously cultivated soil in comparison with continuously cultivated soils and adjacent natural forests soils. For *Cupressus lusitanica* and *Eucalyptus saligna,* they reported an average annual soil C accumulation estimate of 156 and 37 g C m^{-2} yr^{-1} respectively. Their study, which focused on 0–10, 10–20, 20–40, 40–60 and 60–80 cm revealed that reforestation of previous croplands lead to restoration of lost C, even though the differences in deep soils (below 20 cm) were not significant. However, significant difference in soil C was observed in topsoil (0–10 and 10–20 cm) layers in the following order: Natural forest > *C. lusitanica* > *E. saligna* > Farmland. Similarly, Negasa et al. (2017) studied variations in soil properties under different land use types along a toposequence in smallholder-managed farms in southern Ethiopia. Their study focused on three land use types [agroforestry land, cultivated land and grazing land], three slope categories (upper, middle and lower slope) and four soil depths: 0–20 cm, 20–40 cm, 40–60 cm and >60 cm. However, SOC showed significant variation among landuse types especially in top soil layers while agroforestry land use type had higher SOC content and the least SOC content was recorded in cultivated land. These results indicated that SOC content decreased down the slope and the low SOC in cultivated land was attributed to continuous tillage practices by the local smallholder farmers.

In exploring the magnitude of land degradation, estimated soil organic matter (SOM) loss of 1.17–78 Tg year^{-1} from 78 M ha of cultivated and grazing lands was reported by Demessie et al. (2015) in southern Ethiopia. They reported high soil quality index for natural forest and Juniperous procera, and advocated for protection of natural forests from additional accelerated degradation and conversion to other land uses. Increase in SOC storage and decrease in CO_2 emission can be achieved with afforestation and sustainable measures geared towards safe-guarding remnants of the forests. Singh et al.(2010) equally reported similar trend in a study to evaluate soil carbon sequestration under chronosequences of agroforestry and cultivated lands in southern Ethiopia. Specifically, SOC stocks in all chronosequences (12, 20, 30, 40, and 50 years) of traditional agroforestry were higher than the corresponding chronosequences under agricultural lands.

In a meta-analysis to assess the long-term effect of land management on SOC in Ethiopia, Shiferaw et al. (2015) reported that the trend in SOC distribution across different land uses were crop land (CLU), grass land (GLU) and forest land (FLU) corresponding to 1.7, 2.6 and 2.8 g kg^{-1} respectively. However, the variability pattern for SOC was FLU>GLU>CLU, thus the FLU recorded the highest SOC content while the CLU recorded the lowest SOC content. This result agrees with the previous findings of higher SOC storage in natural ecosystems compared with managed ecosystems of continuously cultivated lands (Assefa et al. 2017; Berihu et al. 2017). In reviewing the impact of different soil management practices and land use changes on soil C stock in Ethiopia, Girmay et al. (2008) showed that land use conversion from forest to crop land, to open grazing, and to plantation lead to decline in C stock in approximately 0–63%, 0–23%, and 17–83% respectively at the topsoil layer. The authors proposed adoption of land restorative measures as a panacea to increasing SOC pool. With the adoption of restoration measures, the potential of soil C sequestration ranges from 0.066–2.2 Tg C y^{-1} and 4.2–10.5 Tg C y^{-1} on rain-fed cultivated land and rangeland respectively. The proposed land restorative measures in the form of establishments of exclosures is widely practiced in Ethiopia at the moment but still faces challenges of recurrent trespassing and population pressure on the very scarce land.

With focus on semi-arid area of northern Ethiopia at a watershed level, SOC showed a declining trend with depth within and among most land uses in both magnitude and differential concentrations as reported by Gelaw *et al.* (2014). Dominant soils in the study area are Arenosols, and association of Arenosols with Regosols (WRB 2006). The land uses under consideration were: rainfed crop production (RF), agroforestry based crop production (AF), open communal pasture (OP), silvopasture (SP) and irrigation based fruit production (IR). Their study focused on 0–30 cm depth and showed high potential of SOC sequestration when croplands are converted to grasslands or with the systematic integration of suitable agroforestry trees in croplands. The trend of SOC stock (0–30 cm) were 25.8, 16.1, 52.6, 24.4 and 39.1 Mg ha^{-1} in AF, RF, OP, IR and SP land uses, respectively. Dissimilarities in soil types and management practices across different land uses may have contributed to the variations in C concentrations within the watershed. In investigating the SOC and N stocks of different land use systems along a climatic gradient in northwest Ethiopia, Assefa et al. (2017) reported that 60% of the total SOC stocks were found in the topsoil (0–10 cm). Moreover, clear vertical gradient in SOC stock were observed down the soil profile in forests, considering the following soil depths: 0–10 cm, 10–20 cm, 20–30 cm, and 30–50 cm. With emphasis on Desa'a dry Afromontane forest in northern Ethiopia, Berihu et al. (2017) investigated the impact of changes in land use and land cover on concentrations of SOC and TN sequestration. The study revealed significant difference in SOC distribution among dense forest (2.3%), open forest (1.7%), open grazing land (1.6%), and cropland (1.2%). Thus, higher SOC (44.9 t ha^{-1}) was sequestered in the top soil (0–20 cm) compared to the subsoil layer (20–40 cm). Their findings indicated that the current management practice at the Desa'a forest area is not sustainable and advocates for more sustainable practices to avoid further degradation of the forest remnants. They further indicated that conversion of forestland to other land use might result in huge loss of SOC and other essential soil nutrients.

In view of the foregoing and from the available works on SOC in Ethiopia, virtually all the researchers reported change in carbon pool with soil depth. Change in land uses from forest to cultivated and grazing land leads to appreciable depletion of SOC content. The topsoil was found to sequester more carbon than the subsoil across various landscapes in Ethiopia. Generally, this particular trend was observed across different agroecological zones of Ethiopia irrespective of the soil type. This assertion underscores the importance of adopting sustainable management practices to reduce accelerated release of C from the fragile topsoil. Conversion of grasslands and croplands to forest and exclosures has been found to significantly increase SOC content.

Options for increasing soil organic carbon stock in Ethiopia and in the tropics

It is very imperative to identify and select wide range of feasible approaches that are environmentally friendly and which aim to reduce CO_2 emissions and promote C sequestration. Robert (2006) asserted that effective soil C sequestration can be achieved through the following means: (i) conversion of cropland to forest or pasture/paddock – accounting for 0.5 t C/ha/year average increase; (b) adoption of conservation agriculture and change in agricultural management practices that deplete soil C and overall soil quality– e.g. raised-bed cultivation in arid region, no-tillage, avoiding total harvest by leaving 30% residue or cover crops on the surface of the soil. This assertion is in line with similar studies across different regions of Ethiopia where improvement in C stock has been recorded with conversion of arable and grazing land to forest and/or exclosure (Mekuria 2013; Mekuria & Yami 2013; Assefa *et al.* 2017). Revegetation and afforestation has been recommended as effective approaches for atmospheric CO_2 reduction to ensure C sequestration in both soils and vegetation (IPCC 2007). Restoration of degraded Ethiopian landscapes with the establishment of exclosures and protection of the forest areas for enhanced carbon sequestration potential of soils would enable Ethiopia to partake in the Clean Development Mechanism (CDM). If adopted, this will ensure improvement of the livelihood of the poor smallholder farmers in addition to accruing economic benefits arising from payments for C credits (Carbon Emission Reduction [CER] credits) in conjunction with developed countries.

Conclusion and recommendations

Unsustainable land management practices (deforestation, total/extractive harvesting, uncontrolled grazing, continuous cultivation without fallowing and bush burning) being practiced in many locations in Ethiopia have been found to be key factors in the increased CO_2 emissions in the country. Our findings highlighted massive losses in soil carbon due to forest conversion to other land uses and severe C losses due to agricultural intensification in degraded lands. However, the topsoil layers across different landscapes in Ethiopia recorded higher SOC pool than subsoil, thus underscoring the importance of sustainable land management practices to reduce CO_2 emission from the fragile topsoil layers. The establishment of exclosures by local communities in Ethiopia and continued protection of church forests proves to be a sustainable way of revegetation and land restoration in line with the United Nations Sustainable Development Goals. In addition to establishing SOC long-term field trials which is currently lacking in Ethiopia, current research interest should seek to focus more on the quality rather than only the quantity of SOC stored in different landscapes. This is very essential to our holistic understanding of the status, composition and behavioral dynamics of SOC in the face of changing climate.

References

Assefa D, Rewald B, Sandén H, Rosinger C, Abiyu A, Yitaferu B, Godbold D. L. 2017. Deforestation and land use strongly effect soil organic carbon and nitrogen stock in Northwest Ethiopia. *Catena* 153: 89–99.

Berihu T, Girmay G, Sebhatleab M, Berhane E, Zenebe A, Sigua G.C. 2017. Soil carbon and nitrogen losses following deforestation in Ethiopia. *Agronomy for Sustainable Development* 37: 1.

Demessie A, Singh B.R, Lal R. 2015. Land degradation and soil carbon pool in different land uses and their implication for food security in southern Ethiopia, In Lal et al. (eds.), Sustainable Intensification to Advance Food Security and Enhance Climate.

Resilience in Africa, DOI 10.1007/978-3-319-09360-4_3. Springer International Publishing Switzerland.

FAO. 1986. Ethiopian highlands reclamation study (EHRS). Final Reports, Vol 1–2. Food and Agriculture Organization, Rome.

Gelaw A.M, Singh B.R, Lal R. 2014. Soil organic carbon and total nitrogen stocks under different land uses in a semi-arid watershed in Tigray, northern Ethiopia. *Agriculture, Ecosystems and Environment* 188: 256 – 263.

Girmay G, Singh B.R, Mitiku H, Borresen T, Lal R. 2008. Carbon stocks in Ethiopian soils in relation to land use and soil management. *Journal of Land Degradation and Development* 19 (4):351– 367.

Haileslassie A, Priess J, Veldkamp E, Teketay D, Lesschen J.P. 2005. Assessment of soil nutrient depletion and its spatial variability on smallholders' mixed farming systems in Ethiopia using partial versus full nutrient balances. *Agriculture Ecosystems and Environment* 108:1–16.

Hurni H, Amare B, Herweg K, Portner B, Veit H. 2007. Landscape Transformation and Sustainable Development in Ethiopia. Background Information for a study tour through Ethiopia, September 4–20, 2006, CDE (Center for Development and Environment) University of Bern, Bern.

IPCC, 2007. Climate Change: The physical science basis. Contribution of working Group I to the Fourth Assessment. In: *Report of the Intergovernmental Panel on Climate Change*

(Eds. Solomon, S., Quin, D and Manning, M). (Cambridge University Press, Cambridge, UK).

Lal R., 2004. Soil carbon sequestration impacts on global climate change and food security. *Science* 304: 1623 – 1627.

Lemenih M, Lemma B, Teketay D. 2005. Changes in soil carbon and total nitrogen following reforestation of previously cultivated land in the highlands of Ethiopia. *Ethiopian Journal of Science* 28(2): 99–108.

Mekuria W. 2013. Changes in regulating ecosystem services following establishing exclosures on communal grazing lands in Ethiopia: a synthesis. Journal of Ecosystems. doi: http://dx.doi.org/10.1155/2013/860736.

Mekuria W. & Aynekulu E. 2013. Exclosure land management for restoration of the soils in degraded communal grazing lands in Northern Ethiopia. *Land Degradation and Development* 24: 528–538.

Mesfin A. 1988. The Nature and Management of Ethiopian Soils, Alemaya University of Agriculture (AUA), Ethiopia.

Negasa T, Ketema H, Legesse A, Sisay M, Temesgen H. 2017. Variation in soil properties under different land use types managed by smallholder farmers along the toposequence in southern Ethiopia. *Geoderma* 290:40–50.

Nyssen J, Frankl A, Zenebe A, Deckers J, Poesen J. 2015. Land management in the Northern Ethiopian highlands: local and global perspectives; past, present and future. Published online in Wiley Online Library (wileyonlinelibrary.com) DOI: 0.1002/ldr.2336.

Powlson D.S, Riche A.B, Coleman K, Glendining M.J, Whitmore A.P. 2008. Carbon sequestration in European soils through straw incorporation: limitations and alternatives. *Waste Management* 28: 741–746.

Powlson D.S, Whitmore A.P, Goulding K.W.T. 2011. Soil carbon sequestration to mitigate climate change: a critical re-examination to identify the true and the false. *European Journal of Soil Science* 62: 42–55.

Robert M. 2006. Global change and carbon cycle: The position of soil and agriculture. In: Erosion and Carbon Dynamics. Tailor and Francis Group, London, 3–12.

Shiferaw A, Hans H, Gete Z. 2013. A Review on Soil Carbon Sequestration in Ethiopia to

Mitigate Land Degradation and Climate Change. *Journal of Environment and Earth Science* 3 (12):187 – 201.

Singh B.R, Wele A.D, Lal R. 2010. 19th World Congress of Soil Science, Soil Solutions for a Changing World 1 – 6 August 2010, Brisbane, Australia. Published on DVD.

Stockmann U, Adams M.A, Crawford J.W, Field D.J, Henakaarchchi M.J, Minasny B., McBratney A.B, de Courcelles V.D.R, Singh K, Wheeler I, Abbott L, Angers D.A, Baldock J, Bird M, Brookes P.C, Chenu C, Jastrow J.D, Lal R, Lehmann J, O'Donnel A.G, Parton W.J, Whitehead D, Zimmerman M. 2013. The knowns, known unknowns and unknowns of sequestration of soil organic carbon. *Agriculture, Ecosystems and Environment* 164:80 – 99.

World Bank. 2010. Project Information Document: Kenya Agricultural Carbon Project. http://web.worldbank.org/external/projects/main?pagePK=64283627andpiPK=73230an dtheSitePK=40941andmenuPK=228424 andProjectid=P107798.

Opportunities and Challenges for Integrating Trees in the Irrigated Agriculture Landscapes of Kenya

EDWARD MENGICH, OWINO J., NDUNGU S. AND A. MOHAMED

Kenya Forestry Research Institute

Email: emengich3@hotmail.com

Abstract

Agriculture is the mainstay of Kenya's economy. Due to high population pressure in the high potential highlands, focus is now on irrigated agriculture in the low potential drylands. Irrigation in Kenya has a long history spanning more than 400 years. It involves massive deforestation of the target landscapes, leading to large-scale environmental degradation. Integration of trees to restore vegetation cover would mitigate the impacts of irrigation development. However, information on the opportunities and challenges of integrating trees in irrigated agriculture is not available to facilitate understanding and guide decision making. A survey was conducted in 23 irrigation schemes in Turkana, Baringo and Kisumu Counties of Kenya to gather this information. The schemes were selected based on their socio-economic importance and accessibility. Information was obtained through interviews and interactions with irrigation managers and staff, field visits and observations, and reviews of relevant literature. Key opportunities were; reasonable know-how on tree planting, goodwill from National Irrigation Board (NIB), communities and national and county governments, and availability of irrigation land for expansion. Main challenges included land tenure issues, devolution, un-inclusive policies and inadequate irrigation water. Species/provenance studies, bio-physical interactions research and policy reviews, are recommended among other approaches to enhancing woody vegetation cover.

Key words: Agriculture, drylands, sustainable agriculture, irrigation, agroforestry

Introduction

Agriculture is the mainstay of Kenya's economy, greatly contributing to the country's Gross Domestic Product (GDP) and food security (Kenya National Bureau of Standards (KNBS), 2017). The sector directly contributes 26 % of the GDP, 80 % of formal employment and 60 % of export earnings. It contributes a further 27 % of the GDP through its links with the manufacturing, distribution and service-related sectors. For this reason, the Government of Kenya prioritizes the sector as an important tool for achieving national food security and promoting national development. The country's Agricultural Sector Development Strategy (ASDS) (Government of Kenya (GoK), 2010), for instance, aims at positioning the agricultural sector as a key driver in achieving the 10 per cent annual economic growth rate envisaged under the economic pillar of Vision 2030 (GoK, 2008).

Due to high human population pressure and diminishing land resources in the high- and medium- potential zones, the country is now focusing on the lower potential drylands (KEFRI, 1992) for improvement of national food security. The drylands which cover 80% of the country are home to approximately 4 million pastoralists who constitute more than 10 % of Kenya's population. They also host over 70 % of the country's livestock and 75 % of the wildlife (Orindi et al., 2007). These areas are characterized by low and poorly distributed rainfall, and rainfed crop production is limited by water deficits. Sustainable agriculture can only be achieved through well-planned and operated irrigation. Irrigation is the artificial application of water to assist in the growing of crops, trees and pastures. This can be done by letting water flow over the land (surface irrigation), by spraying water under pressure over the land concerned (sprinkler irrigation), or by bringing it directly to the plant (localized irrigation) (Brouwer et al., 1987).

In Kenya, there are 9.2 million hectares in the Arid and Semi-arid Lands (ASALs) which have the potential for crop production if irrigated. This irrigable area is equivalent to the total farmland in high and medium potential areas in the country (GoK, 2013). Recent statistics show that total area so far under irrigation is 170,000 ha with the National Irrigation Board (NIB) managing 129 irrigation projects distributed in all the 47 counties (World Resources Institute (WRI), 2012). However, government policy direction plans to increase land under irrigation in future (GoK, 2010). A recent development is the Galana-Kulalu irrigation scheme along Sabaki River in Kilifi County (National Irrigation Board (NIB), 2018). By 2016, 4,000 ha of the latter, had been developed for maize farming, and this is expected to increase to 600,000 ha upon completion.

Rationale

Irrigation schemes involve massive deforestation of the landscapes. This, if not well managed, can create large-scale environmental impacts that may negate the expected outcomes from such projects. Replacing trees with shallower rooted pastures and crops leads to an imbalance in the amount of water entering the soil and the amount leaving it through evapotranspiration. Introducing and integrating trees instead, would mitigate the expected impacts on vegetation cover, climate and environmental condition. However, information on the challenges and opportunities for integrating trees in these landscapes that would facilitate understanding and desired decision making is not available. In this regard, information was gathered from irrigation schemes in three counties of western Kenya to understand the socio-economic characteristics of the local people and facilitate future decisions on appropriate tree species, suitable agroforestry configurations, and appropriate component interactions.

Objectives

The main objective of this study was to assess the state of woody vegetation cover and tree planting in irrigated agriculture landscapes and to identify opportunities and constraints/challenges for introducing and integrating trees in irrigated agriculture for decision making.

Materials and Methods

The survey covered irrigation schemes in three of Kenya's 47 counties, namely; Kisumu, Baringo and Turkana (Figure 1). In Kisumu County, field work covered Ahero and West Kano irrigation schemes. In Baringo, it covered Perkerra, Eldume, Kamoskoi, Kapkuikui and Sandai irrigation schemes, while in Turkana, it covered Katilu, Kangarita, Morulem and Turkwel. Also in Turkana, visits were made to rainfed irrigation schemes in Nasinyono, Kakuma, Lokipoto and Lokichogio; Canal irrigation schemes in Kang'alita, Katilu, Morulem, Turkwel, Nanyee and Kaitese, and Drip irrigation schemes in Kaikor and Kachoda.

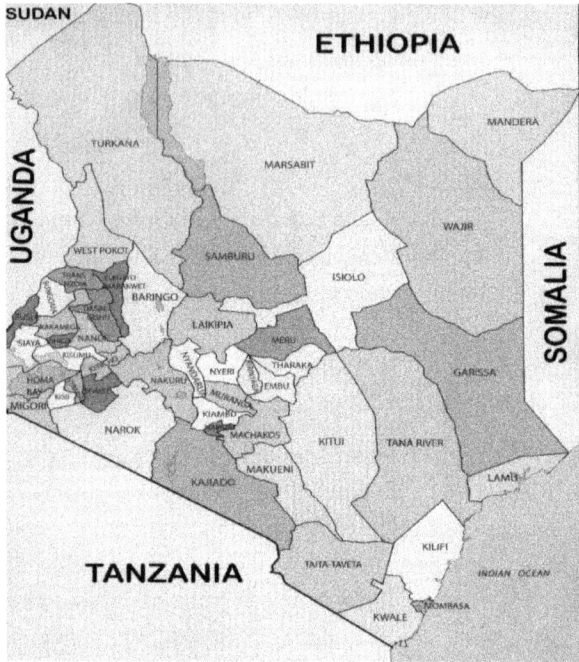

Figure 1: Map showing the counties making up the Republic of Kenya (Source:
https://informationcradle.com/kenya/counties-in-kenya/)

Collection of information involved consultations with irrigation scheme officials,
individual scheme inhabitants, and members of cooperatives and groups within the
schemes. Field visits and general observation of landscapes within and outside the
schemes were also undeertaken. Information was gathered through interviews and
interactions with irrigation scheme managers and staff, observations in the irrigated
fields, and consultation of relevant literature.

Results and Discussion

Natural vegetation

All the irrigation schemes were characterized by limited or complete absence of
natural vegetation (Plates 1 & 2). This was as a result of the woody vegetation clearing
which was done to give way to agriculture.

Plate 1   Plate 2

Plates 1 & 2. Fields clear-felled of woody vegetation at Perkerra and Katilu irrigation schemes

Existing trees were neither maintained nor new ones planted because irrigation managers and dwellers believed that occurrence of trees within irrigation schemes would have negative impacts as follows:

(a) They cast shade on light-demanding crops leading to low crop yields

(b) They provide opportunity for birds to perch close by and feed on the field crops

(c) They absorb large amounts of water, reducing soil water content and increasing drought conditions and crop moisture stress

(d) They obstruct machinery during operations such as de-silting of irrigation canals.

Agriculture

Agricultural activities carried out within the irrigation schemes were dominated by cereals and horticultural crops (Plates 3 & 4). Main crops grown in Kisumu (Ahero and West Kano) were rice, watermelons, tomatoes, onions, soya beans, and maize, among others. In Baringo (Perkerra and other irrigation schemes), they were maize, onions, pawpaws, watermelons, kales, cabbages, bananas, mangoes, avocadoes, citrus, spices and sorghum. Other activities in this area included beekeeping and fishing. In Turkana, crops grown were maize, mangoes, pumpkins, onions, watermelon and bananas.

| Plate 3 | Plate 4 |

Plates 3 & 4. Rice and maize growing in Kisumu and Baringo counties, respectively

Irrigation management

A participatory approach to management was adopted where all stakeholders were involved. They are including NIB, Advisory committees, Local Water Users' Associations, Farmers' Cooperatives, the Ministries of Agriculture, Environment and Forestry, and Water and Irrigation, the National and County Governments, and Non-Governmental Organizations (NGOs).

Sources of water for irrigation included rivers, lakes and boreholes. Irrigation schemes in Kisumu used water from River Nyando (Ahero) and Lake Victoria (West Kano). Those in Baringo used water from Rivers Perkerra, Loboi and Waseges; and those in Turkana used water from Kerio and Turkwel Rivers. In Baringo, some of the irrigation water was obtained from boreholes. The water was distributed by means of electricity- or fuel- driven pumps, gravity and/or both. The cost of pumping is often high and not affordable to many farmers because of the cost of electricity, fuel and maintenance. With gravity flow, the schemes have capacity for expanding the area under irrigation, stabilizing irrigation water flow and reducing the operation and maintenance costs. The water is distributed to the irrigation fields through (a) Main canals (originating) from the source, (b) Branch canals (connecting the main canals to the irrigation blocks), and (c) Feeder canals (draining irrigation water from the branch canals to individual fields).

Tree planting

In all counties, minimal tree planting was observed mainly in irrigation office compounds and homesteads, around villages, and along roadsides. The trees occurred in various arrangements as life fences/hedges, in homesteads and office compounds, along paths and roads, along irrigation canals, in croplands and woodlots and as fruit trees on farms.

| Plate 5 | Plate 6 | Plate 7 |

Plates 5, 6 & 7. Some of the planting arrangements observed in the irrigation schemes

Opportunities for integrating trees in irrigated agriculture

Tree planting not a new phenomenon

Tree planting was observed in various arrangements on farms belonging to people who understood the benefits of tree planting and had the desire to enhance that for sustainable supply of wood products and services. Existence of these trees meant that new trees in new configurations such as fodder banks, home gardens, trees along river banks, improved fallows, and trees on contours may also be introduced with relative ease.

Good will and support from National and County Governments

The performance contract between the National Irrigation Board (NIB) management and the National Government have a component of environmental conservation as corporate responsibility of the irrigation schemes. The irrigation management buys seedlings and supplies them to willing farmers to plant in village plots. The government Farm Forestry Rules 2009 advocate for 10% national forest cover by 2030 through tree planting in areas including irrigated landscapes.

Good will and support from NIB and local communities

This could be observed from the high demand for planting material from both irrigation management and irrigation communities. At Katilu and Nanyee, for instance,

NIB and local communities requested for planting materials of Eucalyptus, bamboo, Grevillea and fruit tree species.

Availability of irrigation land for future expansion

Most of the schemes utilized only a fraction of the total land area originally set aside for irrigated agriculture. In existing irrigation areas, possible target sites to consider for introducing trees are the spaces within and around settlement areas, along riverbanks, and to a limited extend, within the crop fields. Where new irrigation projects are being initiated, the agencies facilitating irrigation development should consider deliberately allocating portions of land for tree planting, and including tree configurations into irrigation plans in consultation with relevant stakeholders and beneficiaries from the onset and in every stage of project preparation and development.

Challenges and Constraints for Integrating Trees in Irrigated Agriculture

a. Land tenure/ownership

Land allocated to families in irrigation schemes is mostly Government trust land where farmers are given tenancy but have no title deeds. Families who do not own the land they occupy have no incentive to plant trees because they are not sure of how long they would be accessible to the land. Legal land ownership provides incentive to plant the trees as owners are sure to benefit from their own trees.

b. Devolved governance

The National Irrigation Board (NIB) which has the legal mandate to manage irrigation schemes throughout the country is a state corporation with a national function. Its function is infrastructural development and expansion of the schemes. The state department of agriculture with mandate to oversee agricultural activities in the schemes has been devolved to counties. The two stakeholders may conflict in the way they wish the schemes run.

c. Invasive species and weeds

Invasion of irrigation water sources and irrigation channels by alien weed species, notably the hyacinth around Lake Victoria and along rivers in Kisumu County, and Prosopis (*Prosopis juliflora*) along Kerio and Turkwel Rivers in Baringo and Turkana Counties. This kind of plant invasion has made construction and maintenance of irrigation infrastructure an expensive exercise because of the costs involved in efforts to control them.

d. Uninclusive policies

The Irrigation Act (1967) (GoK, 1986) which guides activities in irrigation schemes around the country, does not mention anything about tree planting in these areas, neither do the other Acts of Parliament that have relevance to irrigated agriculture landscapes. Absence of such legal frameworks makes integration of trees in irrigated landscapes a difficult task.

e. Livestock browsing and trampling

Although by-laws prohibit livestock from grazing/browsing in irrigation schemes, these are not followed as required. The schemes are mostly not fenced to keep off the livestock; hence the livestock roam around and hinder possibility of tree planting in the schemes. They also destroy canals, drains and other structures. Likewise, households do not fence their homesteads including tree and seedlings, some of which are highly palatable to livestock, hence are not protected.

f. Inadequate irrigation water

Irrigation water across the schemes become inadequate particularly during the dry seasons when stream/river flows reduce due to reduced rains and frequent droughts. Out of the 5,850 acres of the gazetted irrigation scheme area at Perkerra, for instance, only 2,000 acres was cropped due to frequent shortages of irrigation water. Similar observations were made by Keitany et al. (2016) who attributed the annual cropping of only 607 ha out of the possible 810 ha developed for a gravity farrow irrigation system at Perkerra to the limited availability of water.

Plates 8, 9 & 10. Stream and river flows decrease during dry seasons due to reduced rains and extended/frequent droughts

g. Inadequate technical know-how

Although many inhabitants showed some knowledge of tree planting and agroforestry, as well as good intentions to integrate trees in the irrigated landscapes, it was clear that technical know-how was inadequate in some aspects such as tree species choices, planting arrangements, site selection, and tree management practices as demonstrated by field observations. This could be as a result of lack of training, clear guidelines or incentives.

Proposed Way Forward

There is urgent need to address the environmental challenges facing irrigation schemes in Kenya due to clear-felling for cultivation and settlement. Trees can make significant contributions to household food security, environmental protection and climate change mitigation. However, opportunities for integrating the trees should be innovatively exploited, and the challenges/constraints addressed to enhance success of the exercise. Research in areas such as plant species choice, planting arrangements, species-site matching, biophysical interactions, water-use characteristics, and tree establishment and management should be prioritized. Others should include species invasions, legal frameworks, policy provisions, land tenure and capacity building.

Acknowledgements

We acknowledge financial support from the Director, Kenya Forestry Research Institute (KEFRI). Support from National Irrigation Board (NIB) officials through provision of information and guidance during field visits is highly acknowledged.

References

Brouwer, C., Prins, K., Kay, M. & M. Heibloem, 1987. *Irrigation Water Management Training manual No. 5: Irrigation Methods*. FAO, IILRI, Netherlands. Retrieved on 11/1/2019 from: http://www.fao.org/docrep/s8684e/s8684e00.htm#Contents.

Government of Kenya (GoK). 1986. Laws of Kenya: The Irrigation Act (Chapter 347). Revised edition 1986 (1967). Government of Kenya, Government Printer, Nairobi.

Government of Kenya. 2010. Agricultural Sector Development Strategy 2010–2020.

Government of Kenya, 2013. Second Medium Term Plan (MTP II) 2013–2018 of Vision 2030.

Government of the Republic of Kenya, 2008. *Kenya Vision 2030: A Globally Competitive and Prosperous Kenya: Sector plan for Environment, Water and Sanitation 2008–2012*. MENR.

Keitany S.B., Tarus I. & R. Matheka, 2016. Contribution of Perkerra Irrigation Scheme towards the growth of Marigat town in Baringo, Kenya: 1963–2013. *International Journal of Scientific Research and Innovative Technology 3(6): 2313–3759.*

Kenya Forestry Research Institute, 1992. *A dryland Forestry Handbook for Kenya.* KEFRI.

Kenya National Bureau of Statistics, 2017. *Economic Survey 2017.* KNBS, Nairobi, Kenya.

National Irrigation Board, 2018. Galana Kulalu Irrigation Development Project. Retrieved on 11/1/2019 from: https://nib.or.ke/projects/flagship-projects/galana.

Orindi, V.A., Nyong, A. and M. Herrero, 2007. *Pastoral Livelihood Adaptation to Drought and Institutional Interventions in Kenya.* Human Development Report 2007/2008, UNDP.

World Resources Institute, 2012. Kenya GIS Data. Retrieved on 16/08/2017 from: https://www.wri.org/resources/data-sets/kenya-gis-data.

Modeling of Climate Change Impacts on Agrobiodiversity in the Bamenda Highlands of Cameroon

INNOCENT NDOH MBUE

Faculty of Industrial Engineering
Department of Industrial Quality, Hygiene, Safety and Environment
University of Douala-Cameroon

Email: dndoh2009 @gmail.com

Abstract

This study examined the impact of climate change on crop yield in the Bamenda highlands of Cameroon. Twenty-five year climatic data (1991 to date), and crop yield statistic over the same period were collected. Field visits and focus group interviews with 140 farmers purposely selected and complemented the database. The results showed that, on average, while the mean annual temperature of the region increased by 0.04^0C per year, annual precipitation decreased at a rate of about 7.04 $mmyr^{-1}$. The two predictors of climate change, temperature and precipitation explained 43% of the variance in yield (R^2=.43, F (2, 140) =5.56, p<.01). It was found that rainfall significantly predicted crop yield (β = .56, p<.01), as did temperature (β = -.36, p<.01). Declining yields have led to high prices of food items in the market, undermining food security.

Key words: Bamenda highlands, agrobiodiversity, rainfall, temperature

Background

No other form of environmental phenomenon has had widespread detrimental effects on the growth and generative capability of agrobiodiversity as climate change (IPCC, 2012). Manifesting itself through temperature increases, rainfall reduction, new increased pests and disease incidences, droughts and floods, climate change affects agricultural yields in many parts of the world (Lobell *et al.* 2011). This could further result in famine in some food insecure regions (Iizumietal, 2014a).

In response to concerns about the consequences of increase in frequency and severity of disaster events over the past four decades, the concept of community resilience (Mulligan *et al.*, 2016) has gained increasing prominence in science and policy circles. The concept is an essential step toward reducing disaster risk and being better prepared to withstand and adapt to a broad array of natural and human-induced disasters (Burton, 2014). The resilience concept proposes a vision of sustainable development paired with a set of skills to cope with anthropogenic and natural vulnerability including temperature variation and rising input price (Jiggins & Rölling, 2000).

To predict future impacts on crop yields, crop models, for example CERES-Maize (Crop Environment Resource Synthesis), CERES-Wheat, SWAP (soil–water–atmosphere-plant), and InFoCrop (Aggarwal et al. 2006) have been widely used to analyze crop yield-climate sensitivity under different climate scenarios. Although an integral part of rural development, agrobiodiversity has received little attention in the international debate on adaptation to climate change. We suggest that the time series models combined with socioeconomic and environmental dimensions of agrobiodiversity management could provide better predictions of harvest yields at various points in the future.

The purpose of this study is therefore, to model the impacts of climate change on agrobiodiversity using a combination of models, taking the Bamenda Highlands of Cameroon as an example. Specifically the research aims to: (1) Assess the current and future trends in climate change in this region and the relationship between crop yield and climate change data over the past decades, and (2) Conduct a socio-ecological resilience assessment of crops tolerant to climate change related stresses, and a community resilience self-assessment, to understand the ability of the community to cope with threats caused by socioeconomic and physical changes.

Study Area

The Bamenda highlands lies between latitudes 5° 40' and 7° to the North of the equator, and between longitudes 9°45 and 11°10' to the East of the Meridian. It is bordered to the south-west by the South-West region, to the South-East by the West Region, to the North East by the Adamawa Region, and to the West and North by the Federal Republic of Nigeria (Figure 1).

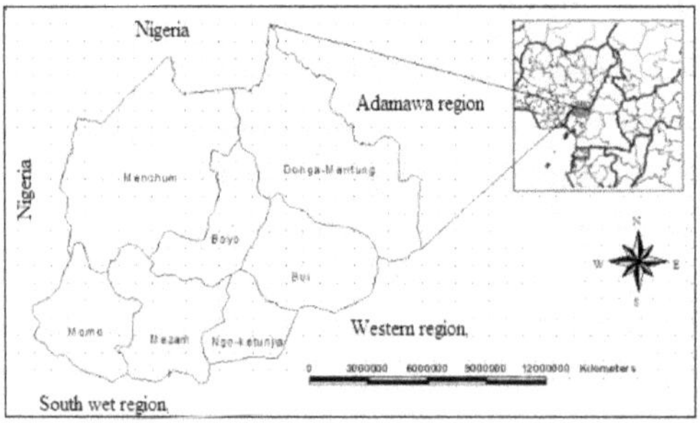

Figure 1. Location of the Bamenda Highlands region, Northwest Province, Cameroon

The region features several dormant volcanoes, including the Mount Oku of all. A cool temperate-like climate, influenced mainly by mountainous terrain and rugged topography also characterize the region. Annual temperature ranges between 150–320C, averaging about 230C, while average rainfall is about 2400 mm (Ndoh and Ge, 2008). There are two main seasons; wet season (April –October), and dry season (November – February). The region is a challenging environment for agriculture due to high interannual variety in rainfall, temperatures and evapotranspiration, poor soil fertility, increasing human population, and the application of resource-depleting and polluting technology.

Methodology

This cross-sectional study solicited the participation of experts and stakeholders in three of the seven divisions that make up the region (Table 1).

Table 1. Sample points: climate stressors, societal impact and sample size

Division	Climate-related stressor	Societal impact focus	Sample size
Mezam	Drought and flood	Drinking water + Habitability+Crops+livestock + fish	50
Menchum	Drought and gas emissions	Livestock + fish	45
Ngoketunjia	Drought and flood	Drinking water + Habitability+Crops+livestock + fish	45
Total			**140**

Key participants were village regents, youth and women's group representatives. Smallholders were targeted because they manage over 80% of the world's estimated 500 million small farms and provide over 80% of the food consumed in a large part of the developing world (UNCCD 2013). The sites were selected to cover a wide range of ecosystems, geographic regions (mountains, plateaus) and climatic stressors (droughts, floods, gas emissions, changing rainfall patterns) as well as dependence of livelihoods on climate conditions (e.g., rainfed agriculture, fishing, herding).

Data Collection and Analysis

Twenty-four year climatic data and crop yield statistic over the same period (1991 to 2015) were collected from secondary database in 2016 from government departments and organizational records. A combination of internet searches and peer reviewed journal articles complemented this database. Field visits, Focus Group Discussion (FGDs) and participatory social-ecological resilience assessment (Bergamini *et al.* 2014) using questionnaires constituted the source of our primary dataset. The FGDs began by asking the farmers to indicate crops they considered had the capability of resisting and adapting in an active way to dynamic changes in both sudden and long-term events. We discussed and scored some key indicators of social-ecological resilience: community assets, institutions, and agricultural practices in four main domains: (1) biodiversity, (2) knowledge and innovation (3) landscape diversity and ecosystem protection, and (4) livelihoods and wellbeing. The indicators were scored on a five-point scale, first by individual participants and then by the group as a whole through consensus, with higher scores indicating stronger elements of resilience. Respondents who perceived climate change were asked which of their crops they perceived to be tolerant and susceptible to the associated stresses based on recall data.

A mixed approach was adopted. Qualitative data obtained from group interviews and field observations were transcribed into descriptive and reflective data that were suitable for converting into useful meaning of units following three procedures suggested by Miles & Huberman (1994). Quantitative data was coded and entered into SPSS 20.0 and both descriptive and inferential statistics were employed to understand how much of the dependent variables (crop species) are explained by the independent variables (temp, precipitation).

Results and Discussions

a. Current and future trends in climate change

Temperatures in the region is increasing at the rate of about $.04°C \ y^{-1}$ and is projected to attain $2°C$ rise in the next 50 years, if everything being equal (Figure 2).

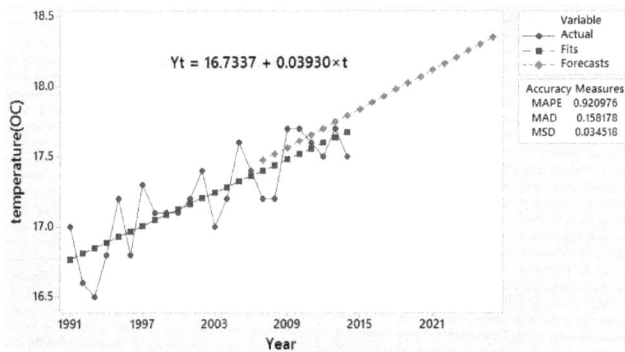

$Yt = 16.7337 + 0.03930 \times t$

Figure 2. Trends in temperature over the past 24 years

IPCC (2007a) projected a temperature increase of between 3°C to 4°C in all four [African] regions and in all seasons, between the years 2080 to 2099. It is safe to assume that temperature change across the Bamenda highlands will follow the general trend for the whole of Africa. Several institutions (for example, UNCCD, 2010) have highlighted that increasing temperature in the course of climate change will result in an increase of desertification rate.

b. Variation in precipitation

Average annual rainfall is expected to decrease drastically below 1200mm per year, decreasing at a rate of about 7.04 mmyr^{-1} (Figure 3)

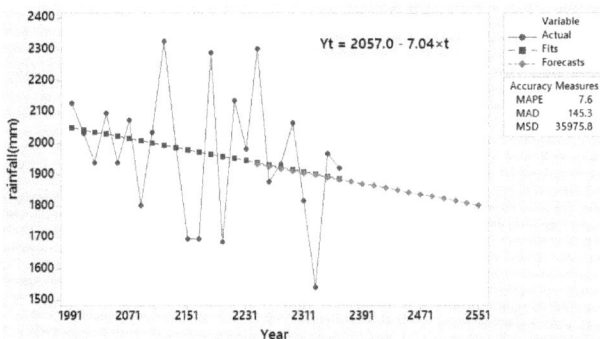

$Yt = 2057.0 - 7.04 \times t$

Figure 3. Trends in rainfall over the past 24 years

The model suggests that the average annual rainfall in the next 24 years may decrease drastically below 1200mm. Our results agree with local perceptions from smallholder farmers. Of the 140 respondents surveyed, 94.27% perceived a change in the weather conditions over the last 24 years. Of these, 82.03% observed an increase in temperature, and 87% observed a change in precipitation patterns. Increasing pest and disease pressure and soil degradation linked to the weather changes by 60.04% and 36% of respondents, respectively.

c. Relationship between crop yield and climate change variables

Evidence of climate impacts on yield was extensive for cocoyams (*Calocasia esculenta*), cassava (*Manihot esculenta*), maize (*Zea mays*), yam (*Dioscorea spp.*) and potato (*Ipomea batatas, and Solanum tuberosum*), but very limited for the rest of the crops. While the yields of all these crops are declining, cocoyams are on a rapid decline and are projected to suffer the largest negative mean change. When the data for different studies were disaggregated, as in figure 4, the wide range of possible outcomes was more clearly visible.

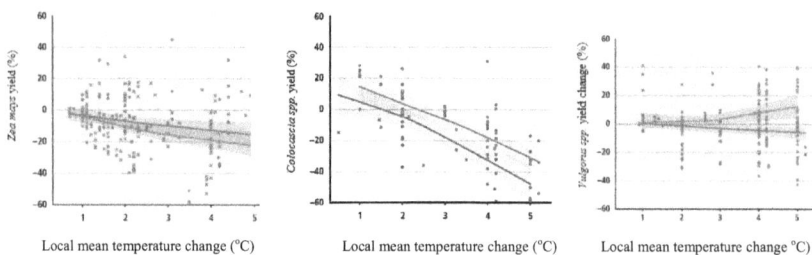

Figure 4. Percentage simulated yield change as a function of temperature change for the three major crops for the region.

The yield of cash crops in the region seem to be affected by key climate variables, temperature and rainfall (Figures 5 & 6).

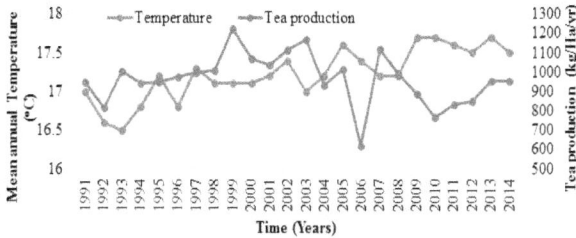

Figure 5. Relationship between annual temperature and tea yield

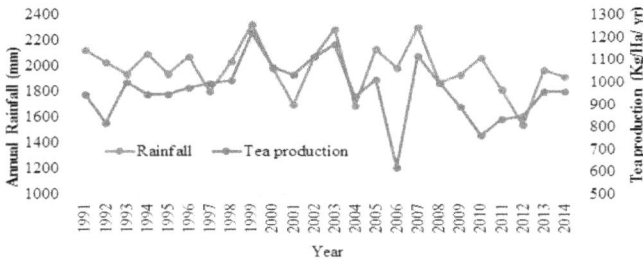

Figure 6. Relationship between tea yield and rainfall

The findings of this study are consistent with those of Avelino et al. (2015), who reported devastated production of coffee in Colombia and Central America due to a combination of factors, including changing climatic conditions.

On the whole, the two predictors, temperature and precipitation explained 43% of the variance in yield (R^2=.43, $F_{(2, 140)}$ =5.56, p<.01). It was found that rainfall significantly predicted crop yield (β = .56, p<.01), as did temperature (β = -.36, p<.01). A one-way analysis of variance (ANOVA) showed a significant effect of climate precipitation and temperature on crop yield, $F_{(2.47)}$ = 7.41, p < .05). Declining yields in turn lead to high prices of food items in the market. For example the price of maize has increased from 15000–25000 FCFA[1] for a 100kg while groundnuts have increased from 42000–48000 FCFA (farmer's voice 2008/12). The situation is expected to expand especially with increase in deforestation, ecologically unfriendly agricultural practices, increase in corrupt practices, limited access to capital and technology and the ongoing sociopolitical situation (Anglophone crises) in the region. Loss of

---

[1] 1USD = 550FCFA

agricultural productivity has been reported to have important impacts on smallholder farmers, resulting in lower incomes, reduced food security, malnutrition and migration of farmers to other areas (Castellanos *et al*. 2012).

d. Perceptions of crops' tolerance to climate change related stresses

About 68 % of respondents in the survey reported suffering yield declines as an impact of climate change. Modelling investigations suggest that some agricultural, forest and aquatic species are more resistant to the effects of climate change than others (Figure 7).

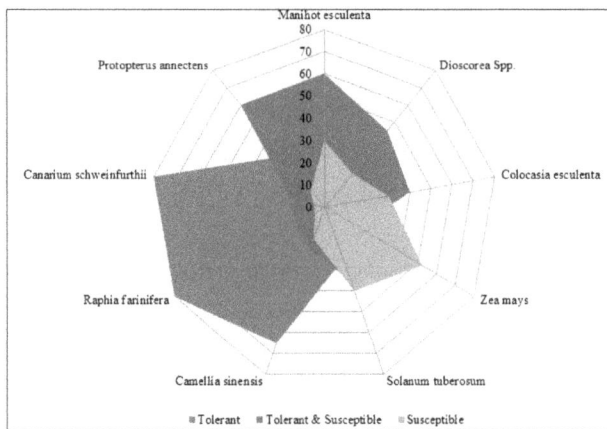

Figure 7. Farmers' perceptions of crop tolerance to climate change stresses in the region

e. Participatory Social-ecological Resilience Assessment

Consensus scores and trends for ten indicators of social-ecological resilience for all the indicators in three domains ranged between (Table 2).

Table 2. Results of the community resilience self-assessment

Domain	Indicator	Consensus score & trend	Explanation for scores & trends
Landscape diversity & ecosystem protection	Landscape diversity	Moderate (2/5) Decreasing	Trees, farms around houses in the landscape and fewer now than in the past. Knowledge of planting does less than 50 years ago. Few protected areas but not sustained
	Ecosystem protection	Low (1/5) Decreasing	
	Landscape integration	Low (1/5) Decreasing	General decline in production services of ecosystems. Adoption of organic inputs in agriculture on the rise.
	Recovery & regeneration of the landscape	Moderate (2/5) Slight change	Extreme temperatures & interannual variations in rainfall retard crop growth, extinction of and loss of biodiversity.
Biodiversity	Crop/animal diversity	Low (1/5) Decreasing	Most animal/plant species are rare. Become available in small populations as one moves away from urban to most rural landscapes.
	Local food diversity	Moderate (2/5) Decreasing	Adoption of improved seed varieties but knowledge is yet to be diversified.
Knowledge & innovation	Innovative practices	Medium (3/5) Decreasing	The community is working with NGOs (e.g. SHUMAS) to improve productivity mainly though organic soil inputs. They are also trying to add value to their products.

	Traditional knowledge related to biodiversity	Moderate (2/5) Decreasing	Decreases from rural to urban areas & in hands of elderly. Fear of traditional knowledge loss as it is not documented and young people are leaving.
Livelihoods & wellbeing	Income diversity	Medium (3/5) No change	Some off-farm works
	Biodiversity-based livelihoods	Medium (3/5) Increasing	Younger people are not interested in biodiversity-based livelihoods, though livelihoods in some forest communities have improved with the help of some development NGOs.

Measuring community resilience is recognized as an essential step towards reducing disaster risk and being better prepared to withstand and adapt to a broad array of natural and human induced disasters (Burton, 2014).

Conclusion

The results of this study provide some fascinating insights into the cognitive and physiological effects of climate change. In line with other studies, agrobiodiversity is under threat of climatic stressors. Agricultural genetic resources are not only a victim of climate change; they are of fundamental importance for adaptation to this change and are crucial to coping with the problems it poses. We recommend a strategic framework for climate risk mitigation in the region. The main objective of the framework will be to define a regional strategic approach to increase the resilience of the Bamenda highland ecological and socioeconomic systems to the impacts of climate change. It is further to assist policy makers and stakeholders at all levels across the grassland area in the development and implementation of coherent and effective policies and measures to climate mitigation. These can be done by identifying strategic objectives, strategic directions and priorities that promote the right enabling environment for mainstreaming adaptation in national and local planning. Moreover it is important to promote and exchange best practices and low-regret measures; promote leveraging of necessary funding, and to exchange and access best available data, knowledge, assessments and tools on climate adaptation.

References

Avelino J., Cristiancho M., Georgiu S., Imbach P., Aguilar L., Bornemann G., Laderach P., Anzueto F., Hruska A.J., & C. Morales, 2015. The coffee rust crises in Colombia and Central America (2008–2013): impacts, plausible causes and proposed solutions. Food Sec 7(2):3030–3321. doi:10.1007/s12571-015-0446-9.

Aggarwal PK, Kalra N, Chander S, et al. 2006. Info Crop: A dynamic simulation model for the assessment of crop yields, losses due to pests, and environmental impact of agro-ecosystems in tropical environments. I. Model description. Agric Syst 89:1–25.

Burton, C.G., 2014. A validation of metrics for community resilience to natural hazards anddisasters using the recovery from Hurricane Katrina as a casestudy. Ann. Assoc. Am Geogr. 105, 67–86.

Castellanos E., Tucker C., Eakin H., Morales H., Barrera J., and R. Díaz , 2012. Assessing the adaptation strategies of farmers facing multiple stressors: lessons from the coffee and global changes project in Mesoamerica. Environ Sci Pol 26:19–28. doi:10.1016/j.envsci.2012.07.003.

International Panel on Climate Change (IPCC), 2012. Glossary of terms in: Managing the Risks of Extreme Events and Disasters to Advance Climate Change Adaptation [Field C.B. et al (eds.)]. A special report of working groups I and II of IPCC, Cambridge University Press, Cambridge, UK, and New York, NY, USA, pp. 557–558.

IPCC, 2007a. Christensen, J.H., Hewitson, B., Busuioc, A., Chen, A., Gao, X., Held, I., Jones, R., Kolli, R.K., Kwon, W.-T., Laprise, R., Magaña Rueda, V., Mearns, L., Menéndez, C.G., Räisänen, J., Rinke, A., Sarr, A. & Whetton, P. Regional Climate Projections. In Climate Change 2007: The Physical Science Basis. Contribution of Working Group I to the Fourth Assessment Report of the Intergovernmental Panel on Climate Change. Solomon, S., Qin, D., Manning, M., Chen, Z., Marquis, M., Averyt, K.B., Tignor, M. & Miller, H.L. (eds.). Cambridge University Press, Cambridge, United Kingdom and New York, NY, USA.

Jiggins, J. & R. Rölling, 2000. Adaptive management: Potential and limitations for ecological governance. International Journal of Agricultural Resources, Governance, and Ecology, 1(1), 28-42.

Iizumi, T. et al. 2014a. Impacts of El Nino Southern Oscillation on the global yields of majorcrops, Nature Communications, 5:3712, doi:10.1038/ncomms4712.

Lobell, D.B., Schlenker, W., Costa-Roberts, J., 2011. Climate trends and global crop production since1980. Science333, 616–620.

Miles, M.B. & A.M. Huberman, 1994. Qualitative Data Analysis (2nd edition). Thousand Oaks, CA: Sage Publications.

Ndoh M.I. & G. Jiwen, 2008. Towards a sustainable land use option in the Bamend Highlands, Cameroon: Implication for Climate Change Mitigation, Income Generation and Sustainable Food supply. Research Journal of Applied Sciences, 3(1):51–65

UNCCD, 2018. White Paper 1: Economic and Social Impacts of Desertification, Land Degradation and Drought. 2nd UNCCD Scientific Conference, 9–12 April 2013

United Nations Convention to Combat Desertification (UNCCD), 2010. Online at http://www.unccd.int/Lists/SiteDocumentLibrary/Publications/Desertification, accessed June 2018.

Conservation in Telecoupled Systems of the African Tropics, Challenges and Opportunities: A Review

EVA W. KIHONGE

Department of Geography and Environmental Planning and Management
Catholic University of East Africa

Email: evakihonge@gmail.com

Abstract

Tropical forests of Africa are at the danger of biodiversity loss due to several factors such as forest fires, illegal logging, expansion of agricultural land and poaching. The main causative factors of all the problems affecting the tropical forests are not only happening locally but they are also generated in other parts of the world and their effects are seen locally. This paper used literature review to find out some of the main flows that contribute to biodiversity change in the African Tropical Forests. A Congo Forest case study was reviewed to shed light on the current status of the telecoupling systems majorly focusing on the tropical forest. Laws and regulations which were introduced to avert further biodiversity loss have contributed to the land use change which has consequently contributed to biodiversity change. The paper concludes that, there is inadequate research to investigate the status of the biodiversity in African tropics.

Key words: Tropics, biodiversity, telecoupling, policies, Forest Stewardship Certification, logging

Introduction

Tropical forests are biodiversity powerhouses since they are home to one half to two thirds of the world's species. Tropical forests are threatened by several factors among them fires, expansion of agricultural land and illegal logging. Food production in the tropics is a major threat to the tropical biodiversity since expansion of cultivation land has led to the encroachment of the remaining tropical forests (Michael et al. 1992, Lewis 2005; Sun et al. 2017).

Tropical forests are found in the zone 23.5^0 North and 23.5^0 South of equator. They are characterized by large trees and they green all year round due to the abundant amount of rainfall they receive. Due to these favourable conditions, the tropics have in the recent times experienced massive changes in the land use systems (Boucher et al. 2011). Conversion of tropical forests to agricultural land has intensified to cater for the rising demand of agricultural products in distant countries, regionally and even locally. Scherr & McNeely notes that 1–5% of the food exports globally, is cultivated in areas where natural forests were converted to cropland.

Complex socioeconomic and environmental interactions between sending systems of the agriculture producing zones and the receiving zones are the major factors influencing land use changes. These interactions are directly linked to the exponential growth of human population and globalization (Tonini & Liu, 2017; Friis & Nielsen, 2017). A multidisciplinary framework is therefore necessary to analyse the flows, processes and the feedbacks that emanate from and within these systems.

Telecoupled systems in the tropics refer to the systems which are shaped by interactions between humans and the environment. Food production in these systems is essential as they provide food which is an important ecosystem service to sustain life (Carrasco et. al, 2017).

Bruckner et al notes that agricultural products used by European Union from 1990 to 2008 were sourced from elsewhere. This is evidence of the increasing biomass trade over distant nations to satisfy demand of agricultural products. Thousands of square kilometres of forest land was cleared in the sender countries to provide land for agricultural expansion (Cuypers et al. 2013; Friis & Nielsen, 2017). Strassburg et al. (2000) notes that the conversion of natural systems to agricultural land is one of the most significant drivers of species extinction.

Demand for agricultural products in faraway countries causes deforestation especially in developing countries located at the tropics where agriculture is the main economic activity. The second largest causative agent of human induced climate change is the conversion of natural systems especially to agricultural land use. It is also the main driver of species extinction (Strassburg et al. 2000).

Without exception, everyone to a larger extent depends on the ecosystem services for water, food and cultural services. It is essential to understand the complete earth system as an integrated whole. Challenges as a result of changes in biodiversity as a result of dynamism in land use should be understood (Lewis, 2005).

Policy makers and members of the civil society ought to view this as an opportunity to address the environmental challenges as they directly cause more societal challenges. This is the ripple effect in telecoupled systems. Humans, oceans, atmosphere and the terrestrial ecosystem interact in an amazingly complex manner (Lewis, 2005). A change in one system or even its component affects another faraway system.

Nonlinear responses are what characterize the changes. Complex feedback mechanisms are observed as well as threshold changes which are critical to understand (Lewis, 2005). Tropical forests are of global importance as they cover 10% of the terrestrial land .They act as carbon sinks which is an important role in reducing human induced climate change. Through photosynthesis and respiration much carbon is stored up in the tropical forests. Tropical forests process approximately six times as much carbon produced by human beings through fossil fuel burning (Friis & Nielsen, 2017).

Most forests in the tropics have evolved to become telecoupled systems meaning that they have become coupled human and natural systems and the interactions are not only local but global. In the world, the tropical forests lie on three principal zones namely Central Africa, South America and South East Asia (Malhi & Grace, 2000). It is noted that all the three zones have experienced rapid deforestation to make way for crop land, pasture land or even logging (Malhi & Grace, 2000). Human interference in these natural systems make them telecoupled especially when the drivers of deforestation are fuelled by international or regional factors such as the increasing demand for agricultural goods.

This paper aims to review the challenges and opportunities in conserving the African tropical forests as components of telecoupled systems.

Telecoupling and Biodiversity Conservation in African Tropics

Land use change is a major driver of biodiversity loss which should be studied using an approach which focuses on distant drivers rather than using a place-based approach. It is following the prominence of socioeconomic and environmental flows which are continuously thriving as a result of food trade flows (Friis & Nielsen, 2017, Meyfroidt *et al.* 2013, Friis *et al.* 2016b).

There is a growing importance of distant drivers of land change as several streams of research have recently revealed. Also, of equal importance are the interconnections between environmental and social systems that have a geographical separation. In tropical forests, the factors which affect land use have a direct impact on the biodiversity. One way in which this happens is when there is a remote market demand, land changes are noted significantly. A demand elsewhere in the world for an agricultural product or a forest resource will prompt increase in the crop land area or massive harvest of the forest product that is in demand and this further aggravates deforestation (Brandt *et al.* 2014).

Environmental policies may act as another driver of deforestation whereby in case a law is changed that favours or acts against deforestation which can be occurred in a faraway country, thus there will be a shift at the rate of tropical forests destruction in the country of investigation (Tonini & Liu, 2017).

China's open door policy which allows them to trade with any country has caused biodiversity loss in Congo Basin. This means that China can directly import timber and forest products from Congo Basin without strict restrictions and this has led to increase of forest cover in China as they continue to satisfy the timber appetite of other countries in Europe and America (Liu & Raven 2010; Liu, 2013).

Liu 2013 notes that the forest cover in China in the last three decades has been increasing. This trend has been attributed to the fact that China has been importing timber and other forest products from other countries (Liu, 2013). One of the countries that china has been sourcing their timber products is Congo where favourable policies like the Congolese Forestry Law of 2000 has encouraged sustainable forest management in harvesting timber for local and international markets consumption. This is a way of revenue generation for the government as well as a sustainable method for satisfying the appetite for timber of international markets in Europe, regionally and even locally (Brandt *et al.* 2014). Such examples are just but a few links between land changes and flows which should be investigated and understood using a multidisciplinary approach.

Congo Basin

A study by Brandt, which used the Congolese Forestry Law of 2000 as a backdrop, noted that the main goal of the policy is to limit degradation of the tropical forest ecosystem by setting standards in logging practices which are based on the sustainable forest management policy. In this case, the policy is an ideal telecoupling example which impacts heavily on biodiversity conservation. As for Congo Forest, the deforestation trend was evident in 1990 where logging took place massively leading to rampant wildlife decline (Maisels *et al.* 2013; Poulsen et al. 2009). It was for this reason that Congo enacted the forest law in 2000 which was meant to document sustainable forest management principles.

In the study on Congo basin, the objective was to investigate a case of telecoupling by capital investments and also how different policies and laws affected the biodiversity change in the Congo Basin. The focus of the study was to find out whether the outcomes of the sustainable forest management laws were in any case influenced by the sources of capital in this case the country which managed a particular forest portion (Putzel *et al.*2011). Further laws on sustainable forest management practices require that the concessions undergo market based certification. In this case forest stewardship certification (FSC) is required which has very strict regulations on biodiversity management. The advantage of the certification is that it draws many customers globally prefer products which are certified as it ensures sustainability (Brandt *et al.* 2014; Putzel *et al.* 2011).

Satellite datasets were acquired and used to evaluate the effectiveness of the policy. Deforestation dataset dating back to 10 years was particularly utilized in the study. Apart from the datasets a quasi-experimental matching approach was used as well to test if in the course of 10 years since the law was passed whether the law influenced the compliance with the sustainable forest management policies as well as the deforestation rates monitoring (Brandt *et al.*2014).

Automated classification was done on the landsat imagery. Two time periods of 5 years each were picked from 2000–2005 and 2005–2010 and maps were made and 12 classes made. As for deforestation, any forest cover loss area was classified as agricultural fields, logging roads and timber extraction areas. To attain a sample size that was computationally feasible, all data was aggregated into 1km grid cell (Brandt *et al.* 2014). Concessionary boundaries were earmarked and this distinguished every investor. The following investors were identified Congo, China, Malaysia, Lebanon and Europe. In summary, simple comparisons were made and conclusions drawn that some management regimes were situated in areas where deforestation was more likely to occur (Brandt *et al.* 2014). The results showed that from 2000 to 2010, most of the actively logged concessions were managed by foreign investor companies. It was noted that deforestation rates were highest close to existing roads, agricultural fields and settlements (Brandt *et al.* 2014).

Concessions owned by the European companies experienced more deforestation. However, they had higher rates of compliance to the sustainable forest management law as compared to other companies. A higher rate of population growth as well as agricultural land expansion has led to deforestation in the Asian and European concessions (Brandt *et al.* 2014).

One of the requirements of the 2000 Forestry law is that the companies that manage the forest provide employment for the Congolese citizens. As a way to give back to the local communities, the companies should either provide basic services to the local communities, ensure that the existing infrastructure is maintained or better still build the onsite timber processing facility (Brandt *et al.* 2014). This has led to increased settlements around the logging concessions and are further expanding throughout the Congo Basin. The highest forest fragmentation pattern was noted around the European owned concessions. All in all the Europeans complied highly to the stipulated and laid down laws and regulations (Brandt *et al.* 2014).

The Congolese Companies had low compliance and was dominated by illegal hence very minimal market incentives. This study highlighted some of the drawbacks which include failure to assess the biodiversity change in relation to the policy implementation. It failed to bring out these important factors so that the necessary measures can be formulated in case there is further decline in biodiversity as it had been noted in 1990s (Brandt *et al.* 2014).

Conservation Challenges and Opportunities in Telecoupled Systems

Due to the interconnectedness in the world, there are conservation challenges and opportunities that exist in the telecoupled systems which exist in tropical countries. Food systems which are located in the tropical forest areas act as major causes for these flows and feedbacks (Adger *et al.* 2009). Below is an outline of the challenges and opportunities summarized.

Challenges

Pressure is mounting on land protection due to high demands of wildlife and agricultural products. This case calls for incentive based approach to conservation. Conservation practitioners have not yet embraced the telecoupling approach to biodiversity monitoring and management (Chang *et al.* 2016). Different interconnections may impact on biodiversity conservation in different parts of the world. These interconnections exist and inform the connection, monetary form, policies and laws, goods and services as well as carbon trade between one distant nation and another. This calls for a management framework can put all these factors in consideration when tackling conservation related problems (Tonini & Liu, 2017).

Opportunities

There are opportunities which exist for conservation practioners and they include the strength of information flow telecoupling to exert strong pressure on governments to ensure that tropical forest are used sustainably and that biodiversity loss is averted (Carrasco *et. al*, 2017). Examples of such a role is the zero deforestation pledges which have been signed by multinational companies like nestle to ensure that their raw materials are sourced from areas which have not been acquired from existing forest area. Another example is the campaign to implement a number of certification schemes which encourage sustainable tropical forest use for example the use of Forest Stewardship Certification (FSC) to ensure that the forest products are acquired sustainably (Ingram, 2009).

Conclusion

African tropical countries need different approaches to conservation which is able to consider all drivers of biodiversity degradation in the forests that are among the few natural ones remaining in on the planet. More research on the distant factors should be encouraged especially on species which are at threatened levels. Each of the species should be established and a comprehensive investigation done to determine the different factors that have contributed to their current status. The African countries lack comprehensive research outlining the current status of the biodiversity that exists in our tropical forests as noted in the research that was done by Brandt. This study reveals a representative case on the current status of most forests in the African tropics.

References

Adger, W. N., Eakin, H., & A. Winkels, 2009. Nested and teleconnected vulnerabilities to environmental change. *Frontiers in Ecology and the Environment*, 7(3), 150–157.

Bonan, G. B. (2008). Forests and climate change: forcings, feedbacks, and the climate benefits of forests. Science, 320(5882), 1444–1449.

Boucher, D., Elias, P., Lininger, K., May-Tobin, C., Roquemore, S., & E. Saxon, 2011. The root of the problem: what's driving tropical deforestation today? *The root of the problem: what's driving tropical deforestation today?*

Brandt, J. S., Nolte, C., Steinberg, J., & A. Agrawal, 2014. Foreign capital, forest change and regulatory compliance in Congo Basin forests. Environmental Research Letters, 9(4), 044007.

Carrasco, L. R., J. Chan, F. L. McGrath, & L. T. P. Nghiem, 2017. Biodiversity conservation in a telecoupled world. Ecology and Society 22(3):24. https://doi.org/10.5751/ES-09448-220324

Chang, J., W. S. Symes, F. Lim, and L. R. Carrasco. 2016. International trade causes large net economic losses in tropical countries via the destruction of ecosystem services. Ambio 45:387–397. http://dx.doi.org/10.1007/s13280-016-0768-7

Cramer, W., Bondeau, A., Schaphoff, S., Lucht, W., Smith, B., & S. Sitch, 2004. Tropical forests and the global carbon cycle: impacts of atmospheric carbon dioxide, climate change and rate of deforestation. Philosophical Transactions of the Royal Society of London. Series B: Biological Sciences, 359(1443), 331–343.

Cuypers, D., Geerken, T., Gorissen, L., Lust, A., Peters, G., Karstensen, J. & H. Van Velthuizen, 2013. The impact of EU consumption on deforestation: Comprehensive analysis of the impact of EU consumption on deforestation.

Friis, C., A. Reenberg, A. Heinimann, & O. Schönweger. 2016. Changing local land systems: implications of a Chinese rubber plantation in Nambak District, Lao PDR. Singapore Journal of Tropical Geography 37(1):25–42. http://dx.doi.org/10.1111/sjtg.12137

Friis, C., & J. Ø. Nielsen. 2017. Land-use change in a telecoupled world: the relevance and applicability of the telecoupling framework in the case of banana plantation expansion in Laos. Ecology and Society 22(4):30. https://doi.org/10.5751/ES-09480-220430

Green, M. J., Murray, M. G., Bunting, G. C., & J.R. Paine, 1996. Priorities for biodiversity conservation in the tropics. World Conservation Monitoring Centre.

Gullison, R. E., Frumhoff, P. C., Canadell, J. G., Field, C. B., Nepstad, D. C., Hayhoe, K., ... & C. Nobre, 2007. Tropical forests and climate policy. Science, 316(5827), 985–986.

Hosonuma, N., Herold, M., De Sy, V., De Fries, R. S., Brockhaus, M., Verchot, L. & E. Romijn, 2012. An assessment of deforestation and forest degradation drivers in developing countries. Environmental Research Letters, 7(4), 044009.

Houghton, R. A., & J.L. Lackler, 2006. Emissions of carbon from land use change in Sub-Saharan Africa. Journal of Geophysical Research: Biogeosciences, 111(G2).

Ingram, V., 2009. The hidden costs and values of NTFP exploitation in the Congo Basin. In *13th World Forestry Congress* (pp. 18–23).

Keys, E., & W.J. McConnell, 2005. Global change and the intensification of agriculture in the tropics. Global Environmental Change, 15(4), 320–337.

Lewis, S. L. 2005. Tropical forests and the changing earth system. Philosophical Transactions of the Royal Society B: Biological Sciences, 361(1465), 195–210.

Lewis SL et al. 2013. Aboveground biomass and structure of 260 African tropical forests. Phil Trans R Soc B 368: 20120295. http://dx.doi.org/10.1098/rstb.2012.0295

Liu J, Raven P.H, 2010. China's Environmental Challenges and Implications for the World. Critical Reviews in Environmental Science and Technology 40, 823–51.

Malhi, Y., & Grace, J. 2000. Tropical forests and atmospheric carbon dioxide. Trends in Ecology & Evolution, 15(8), 332–337.

Maisels F et al. 2013 Devastating decline of forest elephants in Central Africa PLoS One 8 e59469.

Poulsen J R, Clark C J, Mavah G & P.W. Elkan, 2009. Bushmeat supply and consumption in a tropical logging concession in Northern Congo Conserv. Biol. 23 1597–608.

Putzel L et al 2011 Chinese trade and investment and the forests of the Congo Basin: synthesis of scoping studies in Cameroon, democratic republic of Congo and Gabon CIFOR Working Paper 67.

Meyfroidt, P., E. F. Lambin, K.-H. Erb, and T. W. Hertel, 2013. Globalization of land use: distant drivers of land change and geographic displacement of land use. Current Opinion in Environmental Sustainability 5(5): 438–444. http://dx.doi.org/10.1016/j.cosust.2013.04.003.

Scherr, S. J., & J.A. McNeely, 2008. Biodiversity conservation and agricultural sustainability: towards a new paradigm of 'ecoagriculture' landscapes. Philosophical Transactions of the Royal Society B: Biological Sciences, 363(1491), 477–494.

Sun, J., Tong, Y. X., & J. Liu, 2017. Telecoupled land-use changes in distant countries. Journal of integrative agriculture, 16(2), 368–376.

Tonini, F., & J. Liu, 2017. Telecoupling Toolbox: spatially explicit tools for studying telecoupled human and natural systems.Ecology and Society 22(4):11. https://doi.org/10.5751/ES-09696-220411.

Fundamental Role of Frugivorous Animals and Seed Dispersal in Tropical Forest Regeneration: A review

MARGARETHA PANGAU-ADAM

[1]Conservation Biology/Workgroup Endangered Species Conservation, Georg-August-Universität Göttingen, Germany

[2]Biology Department, Cenderawasih University, Jayapura, Papua, Indonesia

Email: mpangau1@gwdg.de

Abstract

The importance of ecological process such as frugivores and seed dispersal in regeneration and restoration of tropical rainforest is overlook. Despite the increasing of deforestation and forest fragmentation in New Guinea, little is known of these ecological processes in forest ecosystem. This paper is a review of the mutual plant-animal interactions especially seed dispersal and the roles of frugivores vertebrates in regeneration of rainforest of New Guinea. Most of vegetation in tropical forest rely on animals for the dispersal of their seeds. Seed dispersal can enhance the mechanism of population dynamics, colonisation and population persistence of forest plants. A number of bird species and volant mammals are considered as major dispersal agents and keystone frugivores in New Guinea lowland rainforest. Many forest plants in this region have relatively large fruits and seeds, indicated the importance of large frugivores such as the ratite birds, cassowaries. Population decline or loss of these keystone frugivores can lead to a failure of seed dispersal processes with long-lasting consequences of forest regeneration.

Key words: Natural regeneration, frugivorous vertebrate, lowland forest, seed dispersal, forest disturbance

Introduction

Because of the high species diversity and endemism, most lowland tropical forests are globally considered as biodiversity hotspots. However, this forest type is seriously threatened across the world, as the increasing human populations require more land and extract more forest resources. The New Guinea rainforest is recognized as one of the last wilderness areas in the world, though rapid development and human population growth in this region are leading to forest exploitation and conversion of its lowland forest (Pangau-Adam et al. 2014). Disturbance from logging operations and large scale plantations mainly palm oil are the major causes of the loss of lowland forest in Papua (Frazier, 2007). Additionally rapid regional development may drive the conversion of forest and landscape to settlements, roads and other infrastructures.

Deforestation and forest fragmentation have become the major threats to the distribution and abundance of many forest biota (Collin *et al.* 1991; Laurance and Bierregaard, 1997; Laurance and Peres, 2006). Since forest fauna play significant roles in rainforest dynamics, changes in their composition in disturbed forest may have consequences for plant-animal interactions and ecosystem processes (Burkey, 1993; Levefre, 2008). A large proportion of tropical plant species depend on fruit-eating (frugivorous) vertebrates for successful reproduction, as these animals disperse their seeds while foraging (Howe 1986; Moran 2007). Therefore, the modification or loss of such interactions in rainforest remnants may have profound implications for forest conservation, especially in the tropics. The extend to which this occurs depend on the diversity and abundance of frugivores and their function as seed dispersers.

Seed dispersal

Seed dispersal is a mutual plant-animal interaction where the animal forages on fruits of plant whose seeds are subsequently transported away from parent plant. In the perspective of frugivores, seed dispersal is called frugivory, and this may be defined as a widespread mutualistic interaction in which frugivores obtain nutritional resources while favoring plant recruitment through their seed dispersal services (Stevenson *et al.* 2015). Seed dispersal is a key process in plant communities and frugivory is very important in vertebrate community (Corlett, 2017). Up to 90% of trees and understorey shrubs in tropical forest have fleshy fruits as an adaptation to attract animals as seed dispersers (Howe 1977; Gautier- Hion *et al* 1985, Corlett, 2017). Seed dispersal by vertebrate fauna has been identified as one of the key components of forest ecosystem. Seed dispersal may play significant roles in maintenance and regeneration of tropical rainforests. This plant-animal interaction can determine the extent and patterns of plant regeneration (Wang and Smith, 2002). It specifically makes an important contribution to individual plant reproductive success, plant population dynamics and the ability of plant species to colonise new habitats (Howe and Smallwood, 1982). Seed dispersal may increase the likelihood of reproduction success of an individual plant by removing its seeds away from the place with highest seed density and seedling mortality (Howe and Smallwood, 1982, Harms *et al.*, 2000). This also increases the plant's reproductive success by delivering seeds to microsites that contain the combinations of abiotic conditions and biotic factors that may improve germination, survival and growth (Hubbell, 1979). Seed dispersal may facilitate ecological processes such as plant colonisation on degraded land and can strongly influence the patterns of plant regeneration on fragmented and disturbed forests (Zimmerman *et al.* 2000; Laurance,

2004, Franklin & Rey, 2007). Furthermore, the interactions between plants and seed disperser agents are important for enhancing succession after deforestation and fragmentation.

Frugivores and forest regeneration in New Guinea

Frugivores or frugivorous animals are animal species which mainly or partly forage on fruits. If they can disseminate the seed of consumed-fruits, they are belong to seed dispersal agents or seed disperser. The main seed dispersers in tropical rainforest are vertebrate fauna (Corlett, 1998). Among frugivorous vertebrates, birds and volant mammals are important dispersal agents because they can disseminate the seeds over long distances and in a large spatial scale. Although frugivorous vertebrates (birds, bats and primates) are distinctive features of tropical rainforests around the world, New Guinea lacks primates and other non-flying frugivorous mammals, and possibly because of this, this region has exceptionally numerous number of frugivorous birds and they fill some of the roles left by mammals (Beehler, 1981). Among the major frugivorous birds in New Guinea are the well-known flightless cassowaries. These avian species are accounted as the world's largest frugivorous birds (Moore, 2007). There are only three species in the family Cassuaridae: the northern cassowary (*Casuarius unappendiculatus*), endemic to central northern New Guinea; dwarf cassowary (*C. bennetti*) an endemic mountain species of New Guinea; and the southern cassowary (*C. casuarius*) occurs in southern part of New Guinea and northestern Australia. All cassowary species are obligate frugivores (Stocker and Irvine, 1983; Moore, 2007) with about 90 to 99 % of their diet dependent on fruits (Bentrupperbaumer, 1997; Wright, 2005). The adult cassowaries maintain permanent and defended home ranges depending on environmental conditions and patterns of food abundance (Moore, 2007). The birds are diurnal and they forage on fallen fruits. They tend to feed on fruit with highly nutritious flesh, avoiding the seeds completely and often with flesh still adhering (Pangau-Adam *et al.* 2015). Cassowaries do not use stones and grit in the gizzard and thus can not access the nutritious seeds (Crome and Moore, 1990). Because of their large-bodied size, these bird species may be able to forage on large fruits and can disperse the large seeds through defecation. Study on fruit variety consumed by southern cassowary indicated the bird consumption on forest fruits of 28 plant species that have large seeds (Stocker & Irvine, 1983). Cassowaries may likely disperse the seeds in different forest types including degraded land which is adjacent to secondary growth forest or primary forest (Pangau-Adam *et al.* 2015). It was reported that the southern cassowary had no site preference for defecation, and a number of dung piles have been collected from disturbed forest sites (Stocker & Irvine, 1983, Pangau-Adam, pers. observation) such as secondary growth forest. The droppings of northern cassowary containing a high number of seeds was observed in secondary forest and forest garden habitats in the northern part of Papua, Indonesia (Pangau-Adam, *unpublished*). Cassowaries may also helpful for the germination rate and successful of rainforest seeds. Seed treatment trials found that cassowary gut passage can significantly improve germination rate from 4% to 92 % of rare forest plants in the northern part of Australia (Webber % Woodrow, 2005). The southern cassowary is efficient disperser of fleshy-fruited seeds and the only major disperser agent of about 100 rainforest plants in north Queensland (Crome and Moore, 1990). Study on frugivores in Papua New Guinea reported that the dwarf cassowary (*Casuarius benetti*) was an important disperser of large-fruited plant species and appeared to be a keystone frugivore for 67 species (Mack & Wright, 2005). Moreover, existing data indicated that the northern cassowary is the primary seed disperser of many plant species of lowland forests in northern part of New Guinea (Beehler, *et al.*, 1995; Pangau-Adam et al, 2015). In New Guinea a high number of endemic plants bearing large size fruits and seeds are dependent on the presence of large-gaped frugivores such as cassowaries (Pangau-Adam & Mühlenberg, 2014). Because of these reasons, cassowaries are accounted as keystone species in tropical rainforest of New Guinea and tropical forest of Australia.

Effects of Forest disturbance

Distribution and abundance of frugivorous birds may be affected through forest fragmentation and habitat loss. Some species showed the sensitivity to forest disturbance, whereas others are tolerant of forest fragmentation (Corlett, 1998; Silva & Tabarelli, 2000; Moran, 2007). Several studies have reported the local extinction of frugivorous bird species in tropical forests following forest fragmentation and extensive forest clearing (Castelletta *et al*, 2000; Ribon *et al.*, 2003, Waltert, *et al.*, 2004). Other studies have compared avian frugivore assemblages in forest fragments and continuous forest and found the abundance of pigeon species higher in continuous than fragmented forest (Date, *et al.,* 1996) and the species number of frugivorous birds in large forest areas was higher than that in forest fragments (Farwig *et al.*, 2006*)*. It was reported that frugivorous birds that specialised on fruit were more sensitive to forest fragmentation than bird species which forage on more than one food type (Castelletta *et al.*, 2000; Moran, 2007). Body size of frugivorous birds may also be the reason of their vulnerability. The home range of southern cassowary is about 2 km^2

(Moore, 2007), means the cassowary may hardly survive in small forest fragments. Distribution of large-bodied frugivorous bird species in fragmented forest was restricted due to their large area requirements as documented in tropical forest of Panama (Sieving & Karr, 1997) and in the rainforest of Southeast Asia (Sodhi *et al.,* 2004).

The conversion of primary lowland rainforests, the main habitats of large frugivorous birds has been considered as one of the major human-induced habitat modification affecting their population range. Study on the northern cassowary in Jayapura region indicated that heavy forest disturbance particularly logging operation reduced the food availability for cassowaries (Pangau-Adam *et al.* 2015). Intensive logging practices are rampant in the lowland forests of New Guinea. The national and international timber companies are particularly harvesting commercially valuable species like the merbau tree (*Instia* spp) (Pangau-Adam pers. observation), a very durable wood type. Timber extraction can destroy the density and vertical complexity of forest structure (Posa & Sodhi, 2006, Levefre 2008) and considerably reduce the habitat quality for frugivores, especially if fruiting plants and nesting trees are harvested. Further effects of logging operations are opening access to wildlife hunters and boosting the increased of hunting activities. Large frugivorous birds are particularly susceptible to hunting. In New Guinea rainforest the large ground-dwelling frugivorous birds especially the northern cassowary and crowned-pigeons have become the major target species for meat consumption and bird trade (Mack and West, 2005; Pangau-Adam and Noske, 2010). Increased hunting pressure in disturbed and fragmented forest may affect large-bodied animals (Sodhi *et al.* 2004) especially large bodied frugivores (Beehler, 1985; Pangau-Adam et al, 2015). The consequences of forest disturbance for frugivorous birds would change the dispersal process of frugivore-dispersed plant species and would be likely to affect patterns of plant regeneration. This may occur due to the changes in species composition and abundance of frugivores in disturbed and fragmented forest (Moran, 2007; Levefre, 2008). Reduced numbers and abundance of frugivores may be associated with lower rates of visitation and fruit removal from focal plants (Bleher and Böhning-Gaese, 2001). Among frugivore species there is variation concerning the quantity of seeds they disseminate (Graham *et al.* 2002) and the temporal period over which frugivores disperse the seeds of forest plants (Greenberg *et al.* 1995). Such variation may also appear in the proportion of seeds that frugivores disseminate to suitable germination microhabitats (Reid, 1989; Murray *et al.* 1993). Accordingly, reduced abundance or loss of frugivorous birds may have impact on the quality, quantity and effectiveness of seed dispersal (Moran, 2007). Disappearance of only few frigivores might not affect seed dispersal as other frugivores could replace the gap (Howe, 1982; Herrera, 1984). However, several forest plants are specialist and depend only on certain frugivorous birds which can not be replaced by other dispersers. For example large-fruited forest tree species are associated with large frugivores and this can not be replaced by small frugivores that unable to disperse large fruits (Herrera, 1984). Loss of these dispersers from their ecosystems could lead to a failure in seed dispersal process (Böhning-Gaese, *et al.* 1999, Bleher & Böhning-Gaese, 2001) and affect the abundance and extinction probability of a series of forest flora (Bond, 1995).

Conclusion and recommendation

Tropical rainforests across the world is seriously threatened, as increased human populations require extensive land forest resources. The mutual interactions between forest trees and frugivorous animals (seed dispersal and frugivory) are fundamental in natural regeneration and maintenance of tropical rainforests. Many forest plants in Papuan lowland forest have relatively large fruits and seeds, require specific dispersal agents like cassowaries that have a large-gape width. Disappearance of these ratite birds through forest disturbance may affect the abundance and extinction probability of a numerous forest plant species that are dependent on the large frugivores. Contrarily, because large frugivores are mostly dependent on the fruits of rainforest trees for their survival (Stocker & Irvine, 1983; Mack & Wright, 2005), loss of their food plant species may lead to the extirpation of these frugivorous birds.

References

Beehler, B., 1981. Ecological structuring of forest birds communities in New Guinea. *In* Gressitt, J.L. (Eds): *Biogeography and Ecology of New Guinea. Monographiae Biologicae*-Volume 42. Junk, The Hague.

Beehler, B.M., Pratt, T.K. and D.A. Zimmerman, 1986. *Birds of New Guinea*, Princeton University Press, Princeton, USA.

Beehler, B.M., Sengo, J.B., Filardi, C. and K. Merg, 1995. Documenting the lowland rainforest avifauna in Papua New Guinea-Effects of patchy distributions, survey effort and methodology. *Emu* 95: 149–161.

Bleher, B. and K. Böhning-Gaese, 2001. Consequences of frugivore diversity for seed dispersal, seedling establishment and the spatial pattern of seedlings and trees. *Oecologia* 129: 385–394.

Bond, W.J., 1995. Assessing the risk of plant extinction due to pollinator and disperser failure. In Lawton, J.H. and R.M. May (Eds.) Extinction Rates. Oxford Univ. Press, Oxford, pp 131–146.

Böhning-Gaese, K, Gaese B.H. and S.B. Rabemanantsoa, 1999. Importance of primary and secondary seed dispersal in the Malagasy tree (*Commiphora guillaumini*). *Ecology* 80:821–832.

Bentrupperbäumer, J. 1997. *Reciprocal ecosystem impact and behavioural interactions between cassowaries, Casuarius casuarius and humans, Homo sapiens: exploring the natural–human environment interface and its implications for endangered species recovery in north Queensland, Australia.* PhD thesis. James Cook University, Townsville, Australia.

Burkey T.V. ,1993. Edge effect in seed and egg predation at two Neotropical rainforest sites. *Biological Conservation* 66: 139–143.

Castalletta, M., Sodhi, N.S. and R. Subaraj, 2000. Heavy extinctions of forest avifauna in Singapore: Lesson for biodiversity conservation in southeast Asia. *Conservation Biology* 14: 1870–1880.

Corlett, R.T., 1998 Frugivory and seed dispersal by vertebrates in the Oriental (Indomalayan) Region. *Biological Reviews* 73: 413–448.

Corlett, R.T., 2017. Frugivory and seed dispersal by vertebrates in tropical and subtropical Asia: An update. *Global Ecology and Conservation* 11: 1–22.

Crome, H.J.1976. Some observations on the biology of the cassowary in northern Queensland. *Emu* 76: 8–14.

Crome, H.J. and L.A. Moore, 1990. Cassowaries in North-eastern Queensland: Report of a Survey and a Review and Assessment of their Status and Conservation management needs. Australian *Wildlife research* 17: 369–385.

Date, E.M., Recher H.F., Ford, H.A. and D.A. Stewart, 1996. The conservation and ecology of rainforest pigeons in northeastern New South Wales. *Pacific Conservation Biology* 2: 299–308.

Farwig, N., Böhning-Gaese, K. and B. Bleher, 2006. Enhanced seed dispersal of *Prunus africana* in fragmented and disturbed forests? *Oecologia* 147:238–252.

Frazier, S., 2007. Threats to biodiversity. In The Ecology of Papua: Part Two (eds A.J. Marshall & B.M. Beehler), pp. 1199–1229. Periplus Editions, Singapore.

Gautier-Hion, A., Duplantier, J.M., Quris, R., Feer, F.,Sourd, C., Decoux, J.P., Dubost, G.,Emmons, L., Erard, C., Hecketsweiler, P., Moungazi, A., Roussilhon, C. and Thiollay J.M. 1985. Fruit characters as a basis of fruit choice and seed dispersal in a tropical forest vertebrate community.

Oecologia 65: 324–337. Graham, C., Martinez-Leyva, J.E. and L. Cruz-Paredes, 2002. Use of fruiting trees of birds in continuous forest and riparian forest remnants in Los Tuxtlas, Veracruz, Mexico. Biotropica 34: 589–597.

Greenberg, R., Foster, M. and L. Marquez, 1995. The role of white-eyed vireos in the dispersal of bursea Simaruba fruit. Journal of Tropical Ecology 11: 619–639.

Harms. K.E., Wright, S.J., Calderon, O., Hernández A. and E.A. Herre, 2000. Pervasive density-dependent recruitment enhances seedling diversity in a tropical forest. Nature 404: 493–495.

Herera, C.M., 1984. A study of avian frugivores, bird-dispersed plants and their interaction in Mediterranean Scrublands. Ecological Monographs 54: 1–23.

Howe, H.F. 1986. Seed dispersal by fruit-eating birds and mammals. In: Murray, D.R. (Eds), Seed Dispersal, pp 123–189, Academic Press, Toronto.

Hubbell, S.P., 1979. Tree dispersion, abundance, and diversity in a tropical dry forest. Science 203: 1299–1309.

Laurance, W. F., and R. O. Bierregaard Jr. (Eds), 1997. Tropical Forest Remnants: Ecology, Conservation, and Management of Fragmented Communities. Univ. of Chicago Press, Chicago.

Laurance, W. F. and C. A. Peres (Eds), 2006. Emerging threats to tropical forests. Univ. of Chicago Press, Chicago

Lawrence, D., 2004. Erosion of tree diversity during 200 years of shifting cultivation in Borneon rainforest. Ecological Applications 14: 1855–1869.

Lefevre KL. 2008. *The influence of human disturbance on avian frugivory and seed dispersal in a Neotropical rainforest.* PhD thesis. University of Toronto, Canada.

Mack, A.L. and D. Wright, 2005. The frugivore community and the fruiting plant flora in a New Guinea rainforest: identifying keystone frugivores. In L. Dew and J.P. Boubli (Eds.) Tropical Fruits and Frugivores: the Search for Strong Interactors, pp 184–203, Springer, the Netherlands.

Mack L.M. and P. West (2005). The Thousand Tonnes of Small Animals: Wildlife consumption in PNG, a vital resource in need of management.Resource management in Asia-Pacific Working Paper No. 61.

Moran, C., 2007. Consequences of rainforest fragmentation for frugivorous vertebrates and seed dispersal. PhD thesis, Griffith University, Australia.

Moore, L., 2007. Population ecology of the southern cassowary (*Casuarius casuarius johnsonii*), Mission Beach, north Queensland. Journal of Ornithology 148: 357–366.

Pangau-Adam, M.Z. and R. Noske, 2010. Wildlife Hunting and Bird Trade in Northern Papua. In: Ethno-ornithology: Global studies in Indigenous ornithology, culture, society and conservation, Eds. Tidemann, S., Gosler, A. and R. Gosford, Earthscan, London, pp 73–85.

Pangau-Adam, M. and M. Muehlenberg, 2014. Palm seeds in the diet of of the northern cassowary (*Casuarius unappendiculatus*) in Jayapura region, Papua, Indonesia. Palms 58: 19–26.

Pangau-Adam, M. and Mühlenberg, M. 2014. Dispersal of Terminalia seeds by the northern cassowary in the lowlands of Papua, Indonesia. Asian Journal of Conservation Biology 3: 115–119.

Pangau-Adam, M., Mühlenberg, M. and Waltert, M. 2015. Rainforest disturbance affects population density of the northern cassowary *Casuarius unappendiculatus* in Papua, Indonesia. Oryx 49: 735–742.

Posa, MRC and Sodhi NS. 2006. Effects of anthropogenic land use on forest birds and butterflies in Subic Bay, Philippines. *Biological Conservation* 129: 256–270.

Ribon, R., Simon, J.E. and G.T. de Mattos, 2003. Bird extinctions in Atlantic Forest fragments of the Vicosa region, southeastern Brazil. Conservation Biology 17: 1827–1839.

Sieving, K. E., and J. R. Karr. 1997. Avian extinction and persistence mechanisms in lowland Panama. In Laurance, W. F. and R. O. Bierregaard Jr. (Eds), Tropical Forest Remnants, Pp 156–170, University of Chicago Press, Chicago.

Sodhi, N.S., Liow, L.H. and F.A. Bazzaz, 2004. Avian extinctions from tropical and subtropical forests. Annual Review of Ecology and Systematic 35: 323–345.

Waltert, M., Mardiastuti, A. and M. Mühlenberg, 2004. Effects of land use on bird species richness in Sulawesi, Indonesia. Conservation 15: 1339–1346.

Wang, B.C. and T.B. Smith, 2002. Closing the seed dispersal loop. Trends in Ecology and Evolution 17: 379–385.

Webber and Woodrow, 2005.Genetic diversity and plant propagation in the rare rainforest tree, *Ryparosa Kurrangii*. A report to the Australian Flora Foundation.

Wright, D., 2005. Diet, keystone resources and altitudinal movement of dwarf cassowaries in relation to fruiting phenology in a Papua New Guinean rainforest. In Tropical Fruits and Frugivores: The Search for Strong Interactors (eds J.L. Dew & J.P. Boubli), pp. 205–236. Springer, Dordrecht, The Netherlands.

Zimmerman, J.K., Pascarella, J and T.M. Aide, 2000. Barriers to forest regeneration in an Abandoned pasture in Puerto Rico. Restoration Ecology 8:350–360.

The Role of Science and Education in Nature Conservation

JOLANTA SLOWIK

Department of Conservation Biology, University of Göttingen

Email: jslowik@gwdg.de

Abstract

There are still some gaps in scientific progress and awareness on global degradation of nature. The global human population in 2018 has reached 7, 6 billion and more than 50% of the land surface has been already transformed by the end of the 20 century through direct human activities, with significant consequences for biodiversity, nutrient cycling, soil structure, soil biology, and climate. Murray Rudd 2011 claimed that conservation scientists are disappointed about the lack of impact their research is having on environmental policies. Effective nature conservation needs good science and scientists working for the cause of nature and truly engaged in protection of valuable species and habitats. The cooperation with universities supports conservation efforts. It delivers the scientific methods and education for anti-poaching units, monitoring teams, helps in elaboration, interpretation of data. Universities educate new generation of conservationists.

Key words: Biodiversity loss, Anthropocene, conservation biology, loss of insects, wildlife, poaching, trophy hunting.

Global change and biodiversity loss

There are some crucial questions regarding future wellbeing of humanity.

How to manage nature conservation and sustainable development in a world of growing human population, ecological and political crisis? What should be the role of science and education for sustainable development and nature conservation? Can science and education help to rescue our planet from destruction and unscrupulous exploitation?

The German politician, and environmental politics expert Prof. Klaus Töpfer was from 1998 to 2006, the executive director of the United Nations Environment Program (UNEP) and 2016, co-chairman of an Independent Team of Advisors on setting the UN development system for the Sustainable Development Goals.

He had come to a conclusion through a graduation ceremony on the 6th May 2017 at the forestry faculty of University of Goettingen that "Scientists exist on finding solutions to problems that former scientists have caused".

The famous scientists Paul Crutzen Nobel Prize winner in Atmospheric Chemistry, Eugene Stoermer, Biologist and Jan Zalasiewicz, Paleo- Biologist insisted that Earth had recently crossed a threshold into a new epoch, the so-called Anthropocene.

The world is changing according to human activities in geologically significant manner and these changes to the Earth system are multiple, complex and interacting (Rockström et al 2009). Over the past two centuries, both the human population and the economic wealth of the world have grown rapidly. The human population in 2018 has exceeded 7.5 billion.

Africa which is now home to 1.2 billion (up from just 477 million in 1980) will by the year 2050, have a total population doubled to 2.4 billion (UN Population Division, 2017).

These two factors – human population and economic growth have led to a massive growth in consumption. Agriculture and food production, forestry, industrial development, transport and international commerce, energy production, urbanization, recreational activities are accelerating. More than 50% of the land surface has been already transformed at the end of 20th century by direct human activities, with significant consequences for biodiversity, nutrient cycling, soil structure, soil biology, and climate.

Over the past three centuries, the amount of land used for agriculture has increased five-fold (Hooke& Martín-Duque 2012). Crutzen (2002), Ellis & Ramankutty (2008), pointed out that more than 75% of Earth's ice-free land area could no longer be considered wild and more than half of all accessible freshwater is appropriated for human purposes. Additionally underground water resources are being depleted rapidly in many areas. The Earth Overshoot day was observed on the 2nd of August 2018 and in the year 2013 it was 20th of August, meaning that humanity is consuming more resources than the Earth can produce (WWF, Ecological Footprint 2017).

The growing human population inducing global change is the driver of escalating biodiversity loss. After UN's 3rd Global Biodiversity Outlook May 2010. Nowadays the rate of extinction of species is estimated to be 100 to 1000 times more than what could be considered natural:

– 75% of genetic diversity of agricultural crops has been lost.

– 75% of the world's fisheries are fully or over exploited.

– Up to 70% of the world's known species risk extinction if the global temperatures rise by more than 3.5°C.

- $1/3^{rd}$ of reef-building corals around the world are threatened with extinction.

- Every second a portion of rainforest, the size of a football field disappears.

The reasons for this disastrous development can be put together in several most important points:

- The increasing world population caused increasing consumption of resources. The interest of individuals and the interest of society as a whole are often opposite and the competitive nature of global economy, with obsession for maximizing economic growth and economization of all aspects of our life are deadly for nature.

- Biodiversity is unquestionable basis of sustainable development and guarantor of human future on Earth. All ecosystem services (i.e. services that directly benefit humanity) depend basically upon the various processes, controlled by organisms, which support ecosystem functioning and maintain ecosystem structures. Biodiversity loss entail erosion of ecosystem resilience (Truchy et al. 2015).

- Biodiversity means the quality of the air, water and soil, productivity of agriculture, horticulture and forestry, provision of goods including food, fibers and medicines, provision of a sink for human waste, ameliorating pollution and prevention of flood. The spiritual well-being and quality of all our lives depend on biodiversity too. Therefore the period 2011–2020 was declared by UN as "the United Nations Decade on Biodiversity".

Unfortunately UNO declarations concerning biodiversity loss are till yet ineffective.

The Living Planet Index (LPI), 2018, as an indicator of the state of global biological diversity, and incorporating 1145 marine, freshwater and terrestrial vertebrate species, demonstrated that between 1970 and 2010, the index fell by almost 40% (Greenfacts, 2018). This LPI Index had been determined by Zoological Society of London (ZSL) in cooperation with the World Wilde Fund for Nature (WWF) and the World Wildlife Fund in collaboration with the World Conservation Monitoring Centre (UNEP-WCMC).

The reaction on biodiversity loss was establishing a new multidisciplinary science called Conservation Biology. This new discipline has the main goal of establishing workable methods for preserving species and their biological communities. Biodiversity conservation is concerned not only with the preservation and management of species and habitats but also with understanding the complex web of ecosystem functions and services and interactions, whether in 'natural' or 'managed' (agricultural, forest, fishery) systems. This requires wide range of methodological and disciplinary perspectives – from spatial and temporal data and models that document and predict ecosystem changes, to the values, governance, political and behavioral contexts which determine the types of interventions that society is willing to implement, and the possibility of their effective management tools such as population viability analysis (PVA). Population viability analysis has been developed to provide "objective" methods for making conservation decisions. These approaches have been key in the transformation of conservation biology from an idea to a discipline (Soulé, 1996).

The big problem of conservation biology nowadays is declining interest on organismal biology, deficiency of ecological knowledge and shortage of data on many species and lack of specialists in taxonomy (Agnarsson & Kuntner, 2007).Taxonomy and population biology are necessary to estimate conservation status of species. The IUCN is working out the Red List of Threatened Species describing the global conservation status of plants and animals on our planet and more than 96,900 species have been already assessed for The IUCN Red List. The new goal of IUCN is to evaluate 160,000 species by 2020. (IUCN 2019) Although the Red List of Threatened Species is not completed, it is still offering the most comprehensive and scientifically precise information about conservation status of species (Rodrigues et al. 2006). A global network for monitoring biodiversity change is necessary to assess ecological state of our planet and create an updated Red List of Threatened Species. A global observing system for biodiversity GEOBON, was created to integrate existing biodiversity monitoring efforts, scattered across regions and countries. The users of this system are ranging from the scientific communities, local communities, and NGOs to national and international policy makers, intergovernmental bodies.Thousands of devoted experts and volunteers from all over the world are gathering the data to make their contributions, in spite of often limited resources, and to warn the society of global biodiversity loss. (Navarro *et al.* 2017)

Science and nature conservation

Science is not static and is changing over time, reflecting transformations in the larger societies in which it is established. Rudd (2011) claims that conservation scientists are disappointed about the lack of impact their research is having on policy. He assumed that it is crucial for conservation scientists to understand the wide variety of ways in which their research can affect policy and be improved systematically.

He described different impacts of research on political decision and actions. Conceptual impact is occurring when policy makers are sensitized to new issues and changing their beliefs or thinking. Instrumental impacts arise when scientific research has a direct effect on policy decisions and symbolic when the use of scientific research results to support established policy positions. It is crucial for conservation scientists to understand the wide variety of ways in which their research can affect policy and be improved systematically.

Nature conservation needs science but unluckily less research is undertaken in developing countries even though much of the world's biodiversity is concentrated in countries with developing economies. Even the investigations carried out in these countries are mostly not guided by local researchers. Scientists from developing countries are also under-represented in important international fora and currently under-represented in peer-reviewed literature (Frazey et al. 2005; Wilson et al. 2017). It is worth emphasizing that the sound, statistically underpinned data warn the societies and politicians against consequences of destructive human activities for years. The societies and politicians are recently informed about massive decline of insects in many countries worldwide. Growing number of long-term studies showing dramatic declines in invertebrate populations insects around the world are in a crisis. Loss of insect diversity and abundance affects food webs and threatens ecosystem services. Even in German protected areas the total flying insect biomass declined more than 75% over 27 years. The loss of insect biomass is responsible for decline in abundance of species depending on insects as a food source in Europe (Halmann et al. 2017). The first international quantitative evaluation of the relative contribution of non-bee pollinators to global pollinator dependent crops (Rader et al. 2015) demonstrated that many of the world's crops are pollinated by other insects as bees which are often assumed to be the most important pollinators. These studies consider the services provided by other types of insects, such as flies, wasps, beetles, and butterflies as important pollinators that are currently overlooked. Furthermore, insects form the base of thousands upon thousands of food chains, and their disappearance is a principal reason that Great Britain's or German farmland birds have more than halved in number since 1970. (Benton et al. 2002, Telfer et al. 2004). Insects are threatened by various pesticides. The use of one group of them, the neonicotinoids, was recently restricted by the European Union. These chemicals bind to the nicotinic acetylcholine receptor (nAchR) in the honeybee brain. Recently, Bayer AG released a new pesticide by the name of "Sivanto" against sucking insects. It is assumed to be harmless for honeybees, although its active ingredient, flupyradifurone, binds receptor nAchR similar to the neonicotinoids. The resent research on effects of the novel pesticide flupyradifurone (Sivanto) on honeybee taste and cognition (Hesselbach & Scheiner, 2018) proved that flupyradifurone can reduce taste and appetitive learning performance in honeybees foraging for pollen and nectar. The consequences of intensification of agriculture on insects are well known and not the lack of research on it but political and economic decisions are mostly responsible for ongoing biodiversity loss. There is no knowledge but there is lack of action.

Sub-Saharan Africa is famous for its wildlife. The big charismatic mammals of Africa are endangered due to growing human pressure. Wildlife population in Kenya's protected areas have declined sharply over the last 30 years, at a rate similar to non-protected areas and became country-wide trends (Western *et al.* 2009). Shrinking of natural habitats, persecution and poaching push many species on the rand of extinction. The killing of lions, elephants and other big games in Africa has been driving highly polarized debates of scientists and conservationists for decades. Trophy hunting certification (Wanger *et al.* 2017) should ensure that sustainability and ethics criteria are met by the trophy hunting industry. Such a system should translate into direct and large-scale benefits for game populations, local communities and conservation funding in Africa. After IUCN African Elephant Status Report 2016, Africa's elephant population has collapsed since 2006 and the relevant cause of this situation is poaching. Fiona Maisels et al. 2013 revealed that population size of elephants declined by ca. 62% (2002–2011), and lost 30% of its geographical range. 20,000 elephants are being killed annually. That number exceeds birth rates, which means that if poaching does not decline soon, elephants could be driven to extinction in the foreseeable future. Illegal poaching and trade of endangered animals has been a huge issue in Africa for many years. Even today, despite great efforts by African wildlife authorities and environmental groups, the killing goes on. Additional killing for pleasure should be in principal prohibited. The legal and illegal hunting affects the animals behavior and can disrupt, for example the elephants' complex matriarchal social structure, reduce their success in breeding. The leading female of elephants is keeping in memory the wisdom of generations. (Burke *et al.* 2008, Paterniti, 2017). Sport hunting is cruel and unnecessary. A small country like Nepal has demonstrated how to ban poaching successfully (Acharya, 2016). It would be very useful for authorities responsible in African countries for implementing anti-poaching actions and to become acquainted with 5 reasons why Nepal is winning the war against wildlife crime.

1. Political push (interest, support, engagement)

The Nepalese government has made conservation a priority, strengthening legal protections for wildlife, enforcing executing rigorous, hard penalties for crimes and forging strong partnerships with conservation organizations like the WWF. It's also streamlined cooperation between its police force, army and park officials, enforcement and monitoring efforts across the country. Nepal's iconic Chitwan National Park, once a poaching hotspot, had more than1,000 patrolling soldiers.

2. Making room

Nepal has set aside an impressive amount of space for nature and 23 percent of the country are conservation areas. According to the WWF, Nepal now boasts of ten national parks, three wildlife reserves and six conservation areas.

3. Implementation technology

The country recognized the potential of new technologies in assisting the fight against poachers early on. Camera traps, satellite radio collars and, most recently, Google Glass have been helping researchers track threatened species like rhinos.

4. Involvement of communities

Nepal's government has taken steps to foster stewardship by giving communities a stake in wildlife conservation. According to the WWF, an estimated 28 percent of the country's forests are now managed by locals. Community Based Anti-Poaching Units (CBAPUs) are active all across the country. Nepal's wildlife reserves receive 50 cents of every tourism dollar earned, so protecting the animals that attract the tourists makes economic sense.

5. International teamwork

The Nepalese government maintains strong relationships with neighboring nations to fight transnational wildlife crime. Presupposition to win battle against poaching worldwide are political willingness and consequent handling.

Education for nature conservation

The position of higher education for the nations and communities plays an essential role for the future. Higher education is recognized as a powerful tool in promoting sustainable development by means of integration of principles and practices of sustainable development into all aspects of education and learning. UNO Global Action Program on education GAP for sustainable development is fundamental and universal in nature and applies to all levels of education (https://en.unesco.org/gap).

The cooperation with universities supports conservation efforts. It delivers the scientific methods and education for anti- poaching units, monitoring teams, helps in elaboration, interpretation of data. The erstwhile Centre for Nature Conservation, Georg-August University in Goettingen had participated in GIZ (formerly GTZ) program of rehabilitation of overused forests in Ivory Coast. This monitoring program for local ecological teams was established and delivered dates were elaborated (Mühlenberg et al.1995). With above half of the world population living in urban areas like cities, the lack of contact with nature and knowledge of species even amongst Bioology students is a serious problem and calls for action. The love for nature, respect for life, interest on species should been learnt from the beginning of education. Education of students should take place not only within classrooms but as well in the field. Important part of education are excursions, practical field work promoting understanding of rules of nature and its functions and demonstrating its beauty.

Nature conservation is an interdisciplinary field of study and research. Georg-August-University offers an integrated bi-national four-semester Master's programme in International Nature Conservation. The degree is a dual degree program offered jointly by Georg-August-University of Goettingen and Lincoln University, New Zealand, and is awared to a graduate as Master of Science (M.Sc.) or Master of Science/Master of International Nature Conservation (M.Sc./MINC).

http://www.uni-goettingen.de/de/information/74766.html.

During this study program, students are learning to contrast and evaluate nature conservation issues and solutions in countries with different biogeographical, human, geological, political, cultural and historical backgrounds.

Statement

Biodiversity is essential for humanity and the escalating and ongoing loss of species could have unpredictable effects on human future. There are some examples of rescue of some species from extinction but with rapid growing human population and increasing consumption of natural resources. In Africa more that 50 % of wildlife are living outside of nature reserves. Some scientists, especially in agriculture sector, describe natural areas as so-called "unproductive land". Ecosystems like the Savanna is not just "unproductive land" but habitat for African Wildlife and African splendour.

Nature conservation can only be effective and practicable with good science and proper education. In our economized and technocratic world, academic teachers are obliged to teach next generation about necessity to save our planet from human incompetence and greediness. It is the last minute to consider Homo sapiens as the center of Universe because we are part of it. Appreciation of nature is anchored in some cultures like Buddhism but globalization, economization of all aspects of life, growing world population, poverty, and socio-political conflicts are responsible for erosion of many cultural and traditional values. As a take home message: 'We cannot achieve sustainable development as long as we are losing biodiversity. Human beings cannot survive without nature'.

References

Acharya, K. A., 2016. Walk to Zero Poaching for Rhinos in Nepal. Department of National Parks and Wildlife Conservation Kathmandu.

Agnarsson, I. & M. Kuntner, 2007. Taxonomy in a changing world: seeking solutions for a science in crisis. *Systematic Biology*. 56, 531–539.

Benton, T.G., D.M, Bryant, L. Cole & H.Q, Crick. 2002. Linking agricultural practice to insect and bird populations: a historical study over three decades. *Journal of Applied Ecology*. 39(4):673–687.

Bouché, F. & P. Bouché, 2016. African Elephant Status Report 2016: *Africa Elephant Specialist Group*. IUCN , Switzerland.

Burke, T., B. Page, G. Van Dyk, J. Millspaugh & R. Slotow, 2008. Risk and Ethical Concerns of Hunting Male Elephant: Behavioral and Physiological Assays of the Remaining Elephants. *PLoS One* 3(6): e 2417 10.1371/journal.pone.0002417

Crutzen, P.J. 2002. Geology of mankind—The Anthropocene. *Nature* 415, 23, 13–18.

Ellis, E. C. & N. Ramankutty, 2008. Putting people in the map: anthropogenic biomes of the world. *Frontiers in Ecology and the Environment*, 439–457.

Frazey, I. J., Fisher & D.B. Lindenmayer, 2005. Who does all the research in conservation biology? *Biodiversity and Conservation*14:917–934.

GEOBON: https://www.earthobservations.org

Hallmann, C.A. R.P., Foppen, C.A. van Turnhout, H. de Kroon, & E. Jongejans, 2014. Declines in insectivorous birds are associated with high neonicotinoid oncentrations. *Nature* 511:341–343.

Hallmann, C.A. , M. Sorg, E. Jongejans, H. Siepel, N. Hofland, H. Schwan, W. Stenmans, A. Müller, H. Sumser, T. Hörren, D. Goulson & H. de Kroon, 2017. More than 75 percent decline over 27 years in total flying insect biomass in protected areas. *PLOS ONE* https://doi.org/10.1371/journal.pone.0185809

Hesselbach, H & R. Scheiner, 2018. Effects of the novel pesticide flupyradifurone (Sivanto on honeybee taste and cognition). *Scientific Reports* 8: 4954

Hooke, R.L & J. F. Martín-Duque, 2012. Land transformation by humans: A review. *GSA Today*, 4–10.

Maisel F et al. 2013. https://doi.org/10.1371/journal.pone.0059469

Mühlenberg, M. J. Slowik, H. Wöll, E .Waitkuweit, 1995. Strategies for restoration of tropical forest that incorporate wildlife protection: an example from Ivory Coast, West Africa.The wildlife society Bethesda, Maryland.

Navarro, L. 2017. Monitoring biodiversity change through effective global coordination. *Current opinion in environmental sustainability* 29, 158–169 www.sciencedirect.com

Niemitz, C., 2018. The present ecological situation of mankind analysis and consequences. *Anthropol. Anz. PrePub-Article J. Biol. Clin. Anthropol*

IUCN Red List of Threatened Species: https://www.iucnredlist.org/

Rader, R. I., Bartomeus, et al, 2015. Non-bee insects are important contributors to global crop pollination. *PNAS* 5, 113, 1, 146–151.

Rudd, M., 2011. How research-prioritization exercises affect conservation policy. *Conservation biology* 25, 5, 860–866.

Truchy, A. D. G. Angeler, R., Sponseller A. *et al.* 2015. Linking biodiversity, ecosystem functioning and services, and ecological resilience: Towards an integrative framework for improved Management. *Advances in Ecological Research* . 2, 53, 55–96

Paterniti, M., 2017. Trophy Hunting: Should We Kill Animals to Save Them? https://www.nationalgeographic.com/magazine/2017/10/trophy-hunting-killing-saving-animals/.

Rockström, J. Steffen, W, Noone, K. *et al.* 2009. A safe operating space for humanity. *Nature* 461, 472–475.

Rodrigues, A. S. Pilgrim, J. *et al.* 2006. The value of the IUCN Red List for conservation. *Trends in Ecology and Evolution* Vol.21, 2, 71–76.

Soulé, M. E 1996. *Conservation Biology: The Science of Scarcity and Diversity*. Sunderland, MA: Sinauer & Associates.

Thomas, J.A., Telfer, M.G., Roy, D.B., Preston, C.D., Greenwood, J., Asher *et al.* 2004. Comparative losses of British butterflies, birds, and plants and the global extinction crisis. *Science*, 303(5665):1879–1881. University of Goettingen: M.I.N.C. 2019. http://www.uni-goettingen.de/de/information/74766.html

UN Population Division, 2017. World Population Prospekts. The 2017 Revision. *ESA/P/WP/248, United Nation*, New York.

UN's 3rd Global Biodiversity Outlook, 2010. UNO Global Action Program on education 2015 to 2019, accessed at: https://en.unesco.org/gap),

Wanger, T. C. W. Lochran, R. Traill, J. Cooney, R. Rhodes & T. Tscharntke, 2017. Trophy hunting certification. *Nature Ecology & Evolution*. 1, 1791–1793 www.nature.com/natecolevol

Western, D. S. Russell & I. Cuthill, 2009. The Status of Wildlife in Protected Areas Compared to Non-Protected Areas of Kenya. *PLOS* https://doi.org/10.1371/journal.pone.0006140

Wilson, K.A. Auerbach, N.A. K. Sam, G.A. Magini, A.S. L. Moss, Langhans, S.D. Budiharta, S., Terzano, D. & E. Meijaard, 2016. Conservation research is not happening where it is most needed. *PLoS Biol.* 14, 3

WWF International, Gland. WWF Global, 2017. *Ecological Footprint.* wwf.panda.org/about_our_earth.WWF Living Planet Report, 2018.

WWF Green facts, 2018. WWF Living Planet Index.

Promotion of Environmental Conservation through Establishment of Environmental Clubs in Primary schools: Lessons from Nyeri County

PENINAH ALOO, MUGO MWARE, MAGRET MWENJE, JOSEPHAT KAGEMA,
DUNCAN KIMUYU, ABDULAHI, MOHAMMED, GREY MAUSI , RICHARD
MATURU, LOICE CHAKA AND N. MURIITHI

Karatina University, Kenya

Email: aloopenina@yahoo.com

Abstract

Environmental degradation coupled with global climate change are concerns world over. This degradation is more pronounced in Africa where poverty has led to massive destruction of forest resources. The rate of destruction of Kenya's forests through human activities is alarming. Currently, the forest cover is estimated at 7.3 % which is way below the expected level of at least 10%. In 2015, the Rufford Foundation and Karatina University supported a project to promote environmental education through establishment of a Botanical Garden at the University and Environmental Clubs in primary schools in Nyeri County. The objectives of the project were to: establish environmental clubs, train the club members on establishment of tree nurseries, sensitize the club patrons on environmental conservation, establish school woodlots and establish a Botanical Garden at Karatina University. To date, the project has established Environmental Clubs in 49 primary schools, sensitized club patrons on environmental conservation and trained club members on how to establish tree nurseries. In addition, the project has established woodlots in the schools, and started the establishment of a Botanical Garden at Karatina University. Besides, the project team have planted trees in three degraded areas in Nyeri County. Other achievements of the project include establishment of collaborations with Nyeri County Government, Kenya Forest Services and National Environmental Management Authority (NEMA) as well as participation in the annual International Day of the Forests. Phase two of the project has just started and another 15 clubs will be established, sensitization of more community members and envisaged near completion of the Botanical garden. The experience gathered in this project demonstrate that young children are the best ambassadors for environmental conservation. Future plans include working with the Government of Kenya, UNEP and other organizations to roll out the project to other parts of the country.

Key words: Environmental conservation, forests, Sustainable Development Goals, environmental clubs

Introduction

Environmental degradation coupled with global climate change are concerns world over. This degradation is more pronounced in Africa where poverty has led to massive destruction of forest resources and consequently to climate change. The manifestations of the change include the rise in global temperatures, unpredictable weather patterns and extreme weather conditions, among others. Climate change alters the ecosystem-human interfaces and interactions that may lead to loss of natural resources and hence erosion of the basic support systems for the livelihood of many people around the world. The main cause of global climate change is the degradation of the environment through destructive human activities.

Our forests are our very existence. If we look after the forests, they will look after us. They have enormous influence on global climate and local weather, sources of food, medicine, raw materials and oxygen, among other benefits. Wangare Maathai, the only Kenyan Nobel Prize Winner once said that *"until you dig a hole, you plant a tree, you water it and make it survive, you haven't done a thing. You are just talking."* Again, Pope Francis once said that *"If we destroy creation, creation will destroy us"*. It is therefore prudent for us to nurture the environment for our own and the survival of future generations. Consequently, under Sustainable Development Goal number 15 on life on land, world leaders committed to "protect, restore and promote sustainable use of terrestrial ecosystems, sustainably manage forests, combat desertification and halt and reverse land degradation and halt biodiversity loss"(SDGs, 2015).

Though the rate of destruction of Kenya's forests has been alarming, the share of forest cover increased from 7.22 to 7.29 per cent in 2017 (KNBS, 2018). Currently, it is estimated at 7.3% which is way below the desired and expected level of at least 10%. The goal of the Kenya Forest Services 2018–2022 strategic plan is to increase the forest cover by 1.15% (KFS, 2017) and Karatina University is a partner.

Karatina University through a project dubbed **Greening Nyeri County** is undertaking activities to green Nyeri County through establishment of Environmental Clubs in selected primary schools in the County. The schools were selected with the assistance of the Sub-County Education Officers in the County. They are distributed in the four sub-counties as follows: Mathira=10; Tetu=6; Othaya=4; Mukurueini=13 and Kieni=16. By establishing Environmental Clubs in primary schools, the project aims to inculcate environmental values in the young children at an early age. This will make them appreciate the benefits from the environment so they can conserve the same. The reasoning behind targeting primary schools is based on the Biblical Principle in Proverbs 22:6 that *"Train a child the way he should go and when he grows up, he will not depart from it"*.

The objectives of the project are to:

1. Establish a Botanical Garden and Nature Trail

2. Establish Environmental Clubs in selected twenty primary schools in Nyeri County

3. Carry out re-forestation in degraded parts of Nyeri County through planting of indigenous trees to simulate a natural forest

4. Use the Botanical Garden and Nature Trail to create awareness on environmental conservation among the youths.

Methodology

The project used purposive sampling method to identify the sample primary schools. A number of factors were considered in selecting the schools including accessibility, distance from the main road and equitable distribution within and between sub-counties. Nyeri County has six (6) sub-counties: Mathira, Othaya, Tetu, Kieni, Mukuruweini and Nyeri Central. For any school to participate in the project, permission was sought from the local Ministry of Education office. After establishment of the clubs, each school was shown how to prepare a seed bed, tree nursery and transfer of the seedlings to the school woodlot. Patrons of the Environmental Clubs were also trained on the same including environmental conservation issues. Karatina University allocated a parcel of land (6 acres) for the establishment of Botanical Garden. An ecological survey was carried out to determine the flora and fauna of the parcel of land before commencement of the establishment of the garden.

Shearman traps (Plate 1) were used to conduct an inventory of small mammals within the Botanical Garden. The traps were baited with a mixture of peanut butter and oats. Further, the presence of large mammals was documented using infra-red motion detector camera traps. Camera traps were baited with chicken wings to lure potential carnivores to the detection zone of the camera traps.

Plate 1. Sherman trap used for small mammal trapping

With assistance from the Kenya Forest Services, degraded areas in Nyeri County were identified for re-forestation.

Results

Distribution of Environmental Clubs

To date, the project has established 49 Environmental Clubs distributed in the counties as indicated in table 1.

Table 1. Distribution of Environmental Clubs in Sub- counties in Nyeri County

Serial Number	Sub-County	Number of Environmental Clubs
1	Mathira	10
2	Tetu	6
3	Othaya	4
4	Kieni	16
5	Mukuruweini	13

Ecological Survey of Flora and Fauna

Results of the ecological survey of flora and fauna revealed the diversity of biota in the botanical garden. A number of plants and animals were reported to inhabit the ecosystem. These include both indigenous and exotic plants and different animal species. Figure 1 shows the diverse plant species in the botanical garden. *Croton macrostachyus, Eucalyptus saligna* and *Neobotona macrocalyx* dominated the plant species found in the garden.

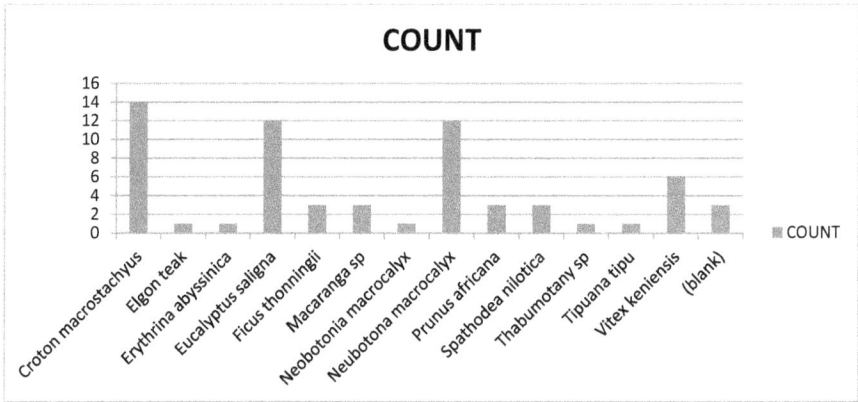

COUNT

Figure 1. Plant species occurring in the Botanical Garden

From a total of eighteen traps, deployed on consecutive days for 9 nights (162 trap-nights), a total of 47 small mammals were captured (29% success rate). The captured small mammals belonged to three different species; *Mus musculus, Crocidura sp* and *Lemniscomys barbarus*

The most common species was the *Mus musculus,* constituting 93% of the total animals captured (Figure 2). Thirty seven percent (37%) of the initially captured individuals (43) were recaptured during the subsequent surveys. All the recaptured individuals belonged to the common species, *Mus Musculus,* hence it was only possible to estimate population size for this particular species. Table 1 shows the number of recaptured individuals per each trapping session. Based on Schnabel estimate, the population size of *Mus musculus* in the botanical garden at the time the survey was conducted was 347 individuals.

Three different species of large mammals were detected within two-weeks continuous period (Figure 2). In addition, there are also anecdotal sighting of black and white Colobus monkey and leopard within the Botanical Garden.

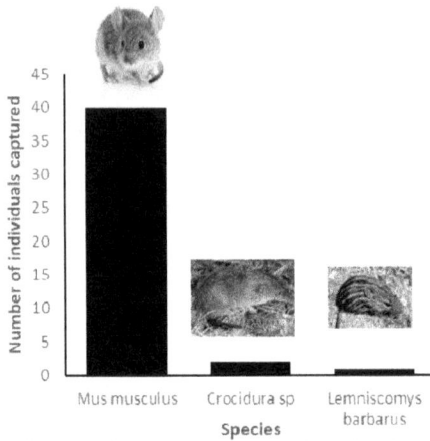

Figure 2. Diversity of animals in the Botanical Garden

Table 1. Number of individuals of Mus musculus recaptured during the nine successive trap nights

Capture	No. of the individuals captured (C_t)	No. of recaptures (R_t)
	No. of the individuals captured (C_t)	No. of recaptures (R_t)
1st capture	2	0
2nd capture	4	0
3rd capture	5	0
4th capture	5	2
5th capture	5	1
6th capture	5	4
7th capture	5	2
8th capture	5	4
9th capture	4	3
TOTAL	40	16

Reforestation of Degraded Areas

Three degraded areas have been planted with indigenous trees to enhance the tree cover in Nyeri County. These are Kieni East at Gatuanyaga (1 Ha), Kieni West at Honi (1 Ha), and Nyeri Central at Muringato (1 Ha). This gives a total of 3 hectares that have been re-planted after degradation. Plans are underway to rehabilitate one more area in Kieni West before the end of the project.

Lessons Learnt

The project has been implemented over a period of three years. During this period, the project team has learnt a number of lessons. These include but not limited to:

i) The project has brought out the fact that environmental virtues are better imparted to children at a tender age because they will grow up with respect for the environment;

ii) Participating schools have owned the project especially after the training of Environmental Club Patrons who have become the champions for the project;

iii) The Government of Kenya is keen on conserving the environment and recognizes activities towards this direction. For example, the Project Team Leader was appointed to the National Environmental Management Authority (NEMA) Board for a period of three years since 2018;

iv) The project opened opportunities for the university to participate in international day celebrations such as International Day of the Forests, World Wetland Day and World Environmental Day;

v) Many primary schools had zoned a place for woodlots but lacked the technical skills to establish a school woodlot. This project has successfully demonstrated the techniques to the pupils and their teachers in the 49 schools;

vi) The project has enhanced University-Community partnerships. Through the establishment of the Environmental Clubs in Nyeri County, we have established partnership with the County Government of Nyeri, Kenya Forest Services, National Environmental Management Authority, Ministry of Education at county level and the community around the University.

Conclusions

With additional support from Karatina University, a Botanical Garden is being established at the University for creating awareness on environmental conservation to university students, community and other youths who visit the Botanical Garden. The project has enhanced partnerships between the University and the Community, County government and other partnering government agencies. This project was ended in April 2019 but there is great potential for expanding the same to more schools within

Nyeri County or to other counties across Kenya. With support from relevant stakeholders, we hope to roll out the project to all primary schools in Nyeri County with each school having a woodlot to enhance the forest cover in the county. Besides, the project team plans to use Nyeri County as a model for rolling out the project to other counties in partnership with the county governments. Finally, we look forward to working with development partners to roll out the project across Kenya in order to enhance the forest cover in the Country to 10% as stipulated in the Constitution of Kenya 2010.

Acknowledgements

We wish to acknowledge the Rufford Foundation for providing funds in two phases to implement this project. Our sincere gratitude to the foundation because the project has opened opportunities to the team members and Karatina University. We are grateful to Karatina University for giving the team time off to carry out the project and providing additional support for the Botanical Garden. We thank our partners including the County Government of Nyeri, KFS and NEMA for believing in us and supporting us in the implementation of the project. We acknowledge the Ministry of Education through the County Director of Education for authorizing the project. Special gratitude to the, the Head Teachers and club patrons of the participating schools and the pupils for their commitment to the project.

References

Kenya National Bureau of Statistics (KNBS), 2018. *Economic Survey 2018*, Kenya National Bureau of Statistics, Herufi House Nairobi, Kenya.

Kenya Forest Service, 2017. Strategic Plan 2017 – 2022, Kenya Forest Service, Nairobi Kenya.

Firzli, M. & J. Nicolas, 2016. Beyond SDGs: Can Fiduciary Capitalism and Bolder, Better Boards Jumpstart Economic Growth? *Analyse Financiere*. Retrieved 1 November.

Njunge J. & J. Mugo, 2011. Composition and succession of the woody flora of South Nandi forest Kenya. *Research Journal of Botany*, 6: 112–121.

Omoro L. M. Pellikka, K & C. Rogers, 2010. Tree species diversity, richness, and similarity between exotic and indigenous forests in the cloud forests of Eastern Arc Mountains, Taita Hills, Kenya. *Journal of Forestry Research*. vol., 21, no., 3, 255–264.

Sustainable Conservation of Traditional Vegetables Species in Central Kenya for Food and Nutrition Security through Involvement of the Youths in and out of School

LOUISE W. NGUGI

Karatina University, Kenya

Email: luwngugi@yahoo.com

Abstract

Conservation of biodiversity by using of traditional vegetables and its existing structures are relevant for sustainability. Biodiversity plays a crucial role in the ecological services such as provisioning, regulating, cultural and supporting of organisms. Youth are an important constituency in conservation of biodiversity. Youth are the back bone of the nation. They can change the future of the society with their well-being, courageous behavior and contribution to key economic systems and nature conservation. Some experts estimate that by 2020, 30 % of all species on earth will be extinct. These review will explore how to enhance conservation of certain five traditional vegetable species in Nyeri County by involvement of the youth through utilization of formal education systems in existence and community structures. The two systems will ensure involvement of youths in school and those out of school. Using schools and community structures ensures sustainability owing to the continuity of those structures. The objectives of proposed review will be to document conservation of traditional vegetables seeds by establishment of gardens in the schools and community. The aim of the review is to source funds to implement the project and to involve youths in agricultural activities by having them tend the schools and community vegetable gardens for sustainability of the proposed projects. Effect of project on other ecosystems services were documented. The review also aims to emphasize the importance of promoting consumption, utilization and conservation of the traditional vegetables species through development of recipes and appropriate agronomic practices.

Key words: Conservation, traditional vegetables, youth, sustainability

Background information

Biodiversity plays a crucial role in the ecological services include provisioning, regulating, cultural and supporting of organisms. Conservation of biodiversity by use of traditional vegetables and existing structures are relevant for sustainability (Francisca *et al.* 2007).

Agriculture is amongst the main pillars of Kenya's economic system and central to the government's development strategy, employing more than 80 percent of the rural workforce in agriculture and processing. Agriculture also accounts for more than a fourth of the country's gross domestic product (USAID 2017a). However, agricultural productivity has been stagnating in recent years due to the frequent droughts, floods, and climate change; thus only about 20 percent of Kenyan land is suitable for farming. Maximum yields have not been reached, indicating the potential for substantial increases in productivity (USAID 2017a).

The percentage of youth in Kenya is about 48% of human population of this country, and in Nyeri County it is about the same. Youth are an important constituency in promoting biodiversity conservation. Youth are the back bone of the nation, and they can change the future of the society with their well-being, spirit and courageous behavior. The following figure 1 shows the age structure in Kenya from 2007 to 2017. In 2017, about 40.47 percent of Kenya's total population were aged of 0 to 14 years.

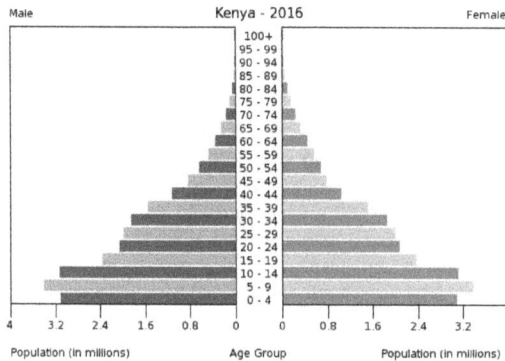

Figure 1. The Population Pyramid of human population in Kenya (Source: Population pyramids net).

Some experts estimate that by 2020, 30 % of all species on earth will be extinct, so action should be taken including efforts to involve the youth (Mavengahama et al 2013; Francisca *et al.* 2007). Unfortunately their involvement in agriculture and conservation biology is minimal and this is also evidenced by low number of students taking up agricultural, biology and related courses in institutions of higher learning.

As human population is increasing, food and nutrient security are fundamental to be improved.

Food and nutrition security status defined as:

"Food security, at the individual, household, national, regional and global levels [is achieved] when all people, at all times, have physical and economic access to sufficient, safe and nutritious food to meet their dietary needs and food preferences for an active and healthy life" (WHO 2012). Food and nutrition insecurity and malnutrition continue to be a global problem meant to have been halved by 2015 millennium development goal (MDG) (Lomazzi, et al. 2014).

One of the main category of malnutrition is hidden hunger and this is including micro nutrient deficiency. Traditional vegetables are rich sources of micronutrients, easily produced and adaptable to local climatic conditions. Utilization of traditional vegetables in Central province of Kenya is still low, although it is one of the most agriculturally productive regions. Domestication of traditional vegetables grow in the region is low (Ngugi, 2004). In a conducted study in Central province of Kenya concerning production trials indicated that the vegetables could easily be incorporated in home gardens (Ngugi, 2004; Okeno et al. 2003).

Methods

The write up of the paper was based on document and literature review. Documents traditional and local vegetable were reviewed and obtained information summarized to the status of traditional vegetables in Kenya among the young people for conservation of biodiversity and food security.

These documented information will also be used to develop a proposal for cataloguing, promotion of production and consumption of local vegetable among the youth in Central Kenya.

Literature review

Status of traditional vegetables in Central Kenya

Traditional vegetables have received little attention in research and development projects. The production of traditional vegetables is low despite their documented benefit for health benefits, food security and as therapeutic foods (Okeno et al. 2003). Kenya is reported to have 210 species of traditional vegetables that are part of diets though not fully utilized (Ngugi et al. 2006, Opiyo et al. 2015). Furthermore traditional vegetables are more commonly utilized in Western and Coast regions of Kenya with other regions referring to them as weeds and having them grow wildly (Maundu, 1997). With increasing awareness on health benefits and increased consumption of traditional vegetables in urban areas the supply does not match the demand, yet this is a significant opportunity for the poorest people to earn as producers and/or traders without requiring large capital investments (Francisca *et al.* 2007; Schippers, 2000). Production and consumption of traditional vegetables is still ow in Central region of Kenya.

Food and nutrition security status

Malnutrition and food insecurity continue to be major global challenges. The potential of traditional vegetables in addressing both have not been maximized (FAO, 2012a; 2012b). Due to their adaptability to local climatic conditions, traditional vegetable have a potential in addressing food insecurity (FAO, 2012b).

Traditional vegetables additionally have health benefits and protecting properties being used for prophylactics and medicinal purposes mostly in the rural areas (Kwenin *et al.*, 2011). These kind of vegetables have been variously used for therapeutic purposes for example by *Solanum nigrum* leaves treat stomach ulcers, abdominal upsets, boils and swollen glands (Opiyo, 2000, FAO/WHO, 2004); The leaves of *Cleome gynandra* concoction may treat scurvy; anemia for pregnant and lactating women (reduces dizziness in pregnant women and eases childbirth). The traditional vegetables non-nutrient bioactive phytochemicals have been linked to protection against cardiovascular and other degenerative diseases. The benefits of these vegetables are maximal when consumed in the recommended amounts (Kwenin *et al.*, 2011). The traditional vegetables if used commercially may provide alternative livelihoods options.

Consumption of traditional vegetables

There exists scanty information about consumption of traditional vegetables despite their health and nutrition benefits and these happened more so for the youths. The reason may likely that some people especially the high income earners consider these vegetables as food for the poor (Lomazzi, 2007). Also majority of these local vegetables are not consumed mainly by the youth of Africans due to their unfamiliar tastes or ignorance of how to prepare those vegetables (Ngugi *et al.* 2003). Urbanization and inadequate scientific information on these vegetables have contributed to low patronage of which knowledge associated with them has been labelled 'backward'. Introduction of exotic vegetables may also have contributed to low production and consumption of African leafy vegetables (ALVs). Association of exotic vegetables with sophistication as well relegates traditional vegetables as backward (Mary, 2007).

The study case

A project focused on the primary schools was to reach the children when they are forming dietary behavior. Total number of primary schools in Nyeri County is approximated 1500 schools. Out of school youths will be reached through youth groups. The study conducted in the region determined the knowledge and consumption of traditional green leafy vegetables among 13–14 years old of youth. It shows that the best known traditional vegetables are *Cucurbita spp* (pumpkin leaves), *Amaranthus spp* (amaranths), *Solanum spp* (black night shades), *Vigna species* (cowpea leaves), *Cleome gynandra* (cat's whiskers) and *Symphtum officinale* (comfrey) in that descending order. Knowledge though by few 10 % was gained through posters and school textbooks. Consumption of the traditional vegetables by the pupils families was by only 5% frequently, 42% averagely and 54 % seldom. Most of the vegetables consumed were purchased from the markets with very little produce by own grown. The main reason for not consuming the vegetables regularly was indicated as their unfamiliar tastes (Ngugi, 2004).

The study has been conducted to document and promote utilization, conservation of traditional vegetable seeds by establishment of gardens in the schools and community. Moreover it was also undertaken to catalogue existing traditional vegetables in Nyeri County, their nutritional and health benefits, as to provide easy access of information for the youths.

References

Mary, A. 2007. The diversity of cultivated African leafy vegetables in three communities in Western Kenya. *African Journal of Food Agriculture Nutrition and Development,* 7:2.

FAO, 2012a. The state of food insecurity in the world 2012, http://www.fao.org/docrep/013/i1683e.pdf.

FAO, 2012b. News article-Neglected crops need a rethink—can help world face the food security challenges of the future, says Graziano da Silva at the international Crops for the 21st Century seminar, 10 December 2012, Córdoba (Spain). http//www.fao.org/news/story/en/etem/166368/icode/

Smith, F.I. & E. Pablo, 2007. African leafy vegetables: their role in the world healthorganization's global fruit and vegetables initiative *Ajfand* 7: 2.

Okeno, J.A., Chebet D.K. & P. Mathenge, 2003. Status of indigenous vegetable utilization in Kenya, *Acta horticulturae* 621(1): 95–100.

KNBS 2010. The 2009 Kenya Population and Housing Census "Counting Our People for the Implementation of Vision 2030".

Kwenin W. K. J., Wolli M. & B.M. Dzomeku, 2011. Assessing the nutritional value of some African indigenous green Leafy Vegetables in Ghana. *Journal of Animal and Plant Sciences.* 10(2): 1300–1305.

Lomazzi, M. Borisch B. & U. Laaser, 2014. The Millennium Development Goals: experiences, achievements and what's next. *World Federation of Public Health Associations, IGH/CMU Switzerland.*

Maundu P. 1997. The status of traditional vegetable utilization in Kenya. In: Guarino, L. (ed.). *Traditional African vegetables.* Promoting the conservation and use of underutilized and neglected crops. ICRAF-HQ, Nairobi, Kenya 1997:66–75.

Mavengahama S., McLachlan M. & W. de Clercq, 2013. Proceedings of the IPGRI International Workshop on Genetic Resources of Traditional Vegetables in Africa: Conservation and Use, 29–31 August 1995, *ICRAF-HQ, Nairobi, Kenya.* pp. 67– 71.

Ngugi I. K., Gitau R. & J.K. Nyoro, 2007. Access to high value markets by smallholder farmers of African indigenous vegetables in Kenya.

Ngugi L.W., 2014. *Development of Information education and communication materials on traditional vegetables among primary school pupils.* M.Sc thesis, The University of Nairobi.

Opiyo A. M., 2000. *Effect of nitrogen application and plant age on edible leaf yield and quality of black nightshade (Solanum nigrum L.) plants.* M.Sc thesis. The University of Nairobi.

Opiyo A. M., Mungai N. W., Nakhone L. W. & J.K. Lagat, 2015. Production, status and impact of traditional leafy vegetables in household food security: a case study of Bondo District-Siaya County-Kenya.

Schippers R. R., 2000. African Indigenous vegetables: An overview of the cultivated species. *NRI/ACP-EU Technical Centre for Agricultural and Rural Cooperation. Chatham, UK.*

WHO, 2012. Trade, Foreign Policy, Diplomacy, and Health: Glossary of Globalization, Trade and Health Terms Geneva: WHO; 2012. Available from: http://www.who.int/trade/glossary.

World Bank, 2010. Distribution Services in East Africa, Regoverning Markets Innovative Practice series, IIED, World Bank forthcoming. Egerton University, London.

Wildlife Hunting on Ground-dwelling Birds in Indonesian New Guinea: A review

MARGARETHA PANGAU-ADAM[1,2] AND HENDERINA J. KEILUHU[1]

[1]Biology Department, Cenderawasih University, Jayapura, Papua, Indonesia

[2]Conservation Biology/Workgroup Endangered Species Conservation, Georg-August-Universität Göttingen, Germany

Email: mpangau1@gwdg.de

Abstract

Indonesian New Guinea is globally known as one of biodiversity hotspot due to its high species diversity and endemism. Around 200 mammal species and 660 bird species inhabit this tropical region. This region is home to around 250 tribes with sets of inter-relationships with their environment. Wildlife hunting has been practised by indigenous people since thousand years, for livelihood and socio-cultural reasons. This paper provides a review on hunting pattern in the past and at present particularly on the ground-dwelling birds (cassowaries and Goura *spp*). It appears that hunting pattern is recently changing from subsistence form to commercial level, and this is likely influenced by the cash market and the movement of migrant communities. Appropriate strategics for sustainable hunting management are fundamental to secure the food sources for local people and to protect New Guinea endemic fauna.

Key words: Cassowaries, endemic fauna, *Goura* spp, hunting pattern, sustainable management, New Guinea

Introduction

New Guinea Island is globally considered as the largest tropical and the second largest island. Biogeographically this island belongs to the Australasia region, which is separated by a shallow sea from the Australian continent. Because of its species richness and high level of endemism, New Guinea is deemed amongst the mega biodiversity regions worldwide. It also has large array of ecosystems ranging from coastal areas to the alpine ecosystems. This large tropical region with its satellite islands is declared as one of three remaining world wilderness areas, besides Amazonian forest and Congo basin. Due to its high biodiversity value and low population density, the Conservation International in 1997 declared New Guinea as "Major Tropical Wilderness Area" (Conservational International 1999). New Guinea Island administratively belongs to two different countries: (1) The Republic of Indonesia (Papua and West Papua Provinces, the largest, yet most remote and least-developed areas in Indonesia), and (2) Papua New Guinea (the eastern half).

The Indonesian New Guinea has been estimated as the home to around 50 % of Indonesian biodiversity (Conservational International 1999), of which are approximately 660 bird species or 6.8% of the globally total bird number (Mack and Dumbacher 2007). This high diversity is partly due to an unrivalled altitudinal range, supporting a vast array of ecosystems from coastal mangroves and coral reefs to montane rainforests, alpine valleys and equatorial glaciers (Petocz, 1989; CI, 1999).

Bird taxa includes the majority of the world-renowned birds-of-paradise, all of the crowned-pigeons, flightless cassowaries, and most of the world's mound nest-builders (Pratt *et al.,* 2015). Bird Life International has identified about 140 Endemic Bird Area's (EBA) worldwide, and eight of EBA sites were located in the Indonesian New Guinea (Sudjatnika *et al* 1995).

As happens in other tropical regions, many bird species and other vertebrates in the forests of New Guinea have become target animals for wildlife hunting and trade. This paper aims to provide a review on wildlife hunting pattern on ground dwelling birds in the forests of Indonesian New Guinea.

Wildlife hunting by indigenous people

Indonesian New Guinea is home to over 250 different ethnic groups, each with rich cultural traditions, languages, and sets of inter-relationships with their environment (Petocz 1989). The indigenous people have a long history of subsistence hunting, fishing and traditional agriculture. Pigs were raised as a source of protein, but in addition, wild pigs have always been hunted, along with other forest species (Petocz 1989).

In New Guinea, local communities traditionally hunt wildlife for meat consumption, as well as for religious and cultural purposes. Hunting has always been one of the most important livelihood activities because it provides animal protein for family consumption (Petocz, 1989; Dwyer & Minnegal, 1991; Mack & West, 2005). Hunting activities in the past was purely practiced at subsistence level.

Moreover, wildlife is important culturally since various animal parts are used as adornments in ceremonies, or as ornaments (e.g. feathers and fur) and tools (e.g. bones and teeth) in daily life (Majnep & Bulmer, 1977; MacKinnon, 1992). Cultural reasons also related to:

1) Private collection to show hunters' status or pride, for example through collections of skulls, feathers, horns, leathers, claws and preserved animals (Kwapena 1984, Petocz 1978, Aiyadurai 2011),

2) Having a high reputation or certain status/position in tribe hierarchy, that can be achieved through hunters ability and success. The lattest can lead to obtain a kind of competency to marry a woman (Kwapena 1984, Pattiselano 2003, Aiyadurai et al 2010).

In general, New Guinean people consider that forest is like a mother to them, and they rely on plants and wild animals in forest for food source, clothes and shelters, and also for other cultural purposes (Kwapena 1984; Pattiselano 2003). In addition, certain animals are part of the traditional belief systems of many ethnic groups (Majnep & Bulmer 1977; Caldecott, 1995; Pangau-Adam & Noske, 2010).

Although there have been many studies of hunting in New Guinea (see Cuthbert 2009 for summary), most are from an anthropological perspective and done in Papua New Guinea (Pangau-Adam *et al.* 2012). Only few studies have been undertaken in Indonesian New Guinea.

Prior to the western contact, New Guinean people pursued wildlife hunting for subsistence purposes. Until now this hunting pattern can still be found in remote and isolated villages which are inhabited by indigenous people, and where there is no market and ease access to the towns (Pangau Adam 2017, pers. observation). Local people in these villages are totally forest-dependent and wildlife hunting is pursued in a regular basis. Large sized birds such as cassowaries are reared and when it reached adult age, all villagers will consume it together during village event or traditional ceremonies. However, the introduction of a cash market economy, combined with rapid urban and infrastructure development in Indonesian New Guinea and transmigration programs, have became causative factors for the significant change in hunting patterns. Recent study documented, only 26% of interviewed hunters declared that they hunted mainly for subsistence purposes, showing that there has been a marked shift from local-level subsistence hunting for meat consumption towards more intensive commercial hunting (Pangau-Adam & Noske, 2010). Consequently, local communities now view wildlife as a significant source of income. Family heads often viewed hunting as a way to meet the family's livelihood needs and to provide financial support for their schoolchildren. Although most hunters also grew crops, hunting was viewed as a way to obtain immediate cash throughout the year, as opposed to the possibly higher but only seasonal economic benefits from agriculture (Pangau-Adam

& Noske, 2010). The transmigrant communities (people from other Indonesian islands) prefer to capture wild animals specifically endemic forest birds for commercial purposes to meet the demand of local, national and even international wildlife markets.

Local communities living closed to the forest and rather far from towns have high consumption of wild animals than other food items. Study on wildlife hunting in remote villages in Jayapura region reported, that wild meat appeared to be the most prevalent source of animal protein in the seven villages sampled (Pangau-Adam et al. 2012). From the total of 546 records of meals, it was found that the percentage of meals containing wild meat (around 51) was greater than those containing fish (17.4%), domestic animals (13.7%), vegetables (16.0%) and/or other food items (1.8%). Subsistence hunters pursue hunting to satisfy the protein needs of their families, while commercial hunters captured and sold wild animals for cash. However, heads, legs and intestines of killed animals were typically removed (~1–5 kg per animal) for family consumption prior to transporting the prime meat cuts to the market or selling it in the village.

In the past the main hunting technique was using bow-and-arrow. Currently hunters have developed different strategies and used a variety of hunting techniques. Hunting with bow-and-arrow and snares using cable or natural materials such as liana were the predominant hunting techniques, used in over 70% of hunts (Pangau-Adam et al. 2012). The other methods are using dog, gun and catapults. The use of cable snares in Papua is considered as the influence of transmigrant groups. Snare trapping can result in high rates of wasted captures (Lee, 2000; Noss, 2000). Most hunters in Jayapura region were well aware of how long animals could survive in a snare, yet many animals still died in snares long before the hunter arrived because they did not patrol snare lines on a daily basis (Pangau-Adam and Noske, 2010). Air rifles were introduced to the trading town by transmigrant groups from other Indonesian islands particularly from Java and South Sulawesi. Both local people and transmigrant settlers preffer to use this weapon to hunt Birds of Paradise, cockaatos, cuscusses and flying foxes. Due to the high cost of air rifles and cartridges, however, relatively few hunters used this method of hunting.

Hunting on ground-dwelling birds

New Guinea differs from other tropical rainforest regions of the world in having few large native game species. Amongst them are the largest flightless birds cassowaries

(Casuariidae; 25–60 kg) and ground-dwelling crowned pigeons (*Goura* spp). As these few large animals provide the highest protein reward, they are usually the first to be extirpated from forests close to villages (e.g. King & Nijboer, 1994; BirdLife International, 2000; Richards & Suryadi, 2000).

Globally there are only three species in the family Cassuaridae, and two of them (the northern cassowary *Casuarius unappendiculatus* and dwarf cassowary *Casuarius bennetti* are endemic to the New Guinea. The southern cassowary *Casuarius casuarius* is a native species in southern New Guinea and the northern part of Australia. Cassowaries play a fundamental role in seed dispersal of numerous forest plants and have been considered as keystone species in forest ecosystems of New Guinea and Australia (Crome & Moore, 1990; Mack & Wright, 2005; Pangau-adam *et al.* 2015).

The other New Guinean ground-dwelling birds with large body size are *Goura* spp, considered as the largest pigeons in the world. Similar to the cassowaries, worldwide there are only three species in the genus Goura; the Western crowned pigeon *Goura cristata* inhabits lowland areas of the Vogelkop Peninsula, the Scheepmaker's crowned pigeon *Goura scheepmakeri* occurs in the southern lowlands, and the Victoria crowned pigeon *Goura victoria* occupies the lowland forests of the northern New Guinea. All three species are considered by IUCN as Vulnerable to extinction through hunting, and are listed on Appendix II of CITES (Statterfields *et al.* 1998).

Actually cassowaries and crowned pigeons have been declared as protected species by the Indonesian Government (Government of Indonesia, Regulation No 7, 1999). However, bird hunting and collecting of their eggs are still common in many regions of Indonesian New Guinea (Pangau-Adam, pers. observation). These birds are primarily killed for food, although its feathers are sometimes used for head-dresses (Coates 1985), and nestlings are also taken to be reared for food and pets (Birdlife International 2000, Pangau-Adam & Noske 2010). The biodiversity conservation priority-setting workshop in Papua in 1997 has identified that illegal bird hunting and trade were the major threats to birds of New Guinea (Conservation International, 1999). The large ground-dwelling forest birds especially cassowaries and *Goura* spp are particularly susceptible to hunting with snare traps (Pangau-Adam & Noske, 2010). Due to their large body size, the northern cassowary and Victoria crowned pigeons have become the main target bird species for meat consumption among Genyem people in Jayapura Regency, and its meat was frequently traded in local markets (Pangau-Adam & Noske, 2010).

Furthermore, rapid developmen and logging operations provided infrastructure for hunters to access the remote forest areas. Supported by new established markets, these may drive the increased of number of hunters and hunting activities. As a result, more wildlife is captured for commercial purposes. Recent analyses of hunting and capture rates, combined with estimates of population densities and rates of increase indicated that the offtake rates of cassowaries and several frequently hunted medium-sized mammals are unsustainable (Johnson *et al.* 2004; Cuthbert, 2010). As the consequences, eleven of the 14 species of tree-kangaroos (*Dendrolagus* spp.), most of them endemic to New Guinea, and two of the three cassowaries, are now considered threatened with, or vulnerable to, extinction, principally due to wildlife hunting (Stattersfield *et al.* 1998; IUCN, 2010; Pangau-Adam *et al.* 2012).

Due to its large size, hunters also collected the eggs of cassowaries for own consumption or selling them in the markets. Crafting are also done on cassowary's eggshells and the products have become attractive souveniers.

Figure 1. The egg of northern cassowary, measure about 8 by 14 cm is the third avian largest egg (after ostrich and emu eggs).

Figure 2. The northern cassowary is amongst the main target species of wildlife hunting in Indonesian New Guinea.

As for the traditional belief and cultural reasons, some local communities ban hunting practices on certain forest bird species. They believed wild animals such as cassowaries, birds of paradise, and cuscuses are their ancestral, and hunting them might cause such catastrophal consequences. However, in the recent transition and modernization era faced, the traditional beliefs are gradually disappearing. Particular studies and efforts on strengthening and guidance the existing traditional institutions are critical to minimized or avoid over-exploitation on ground-dwelling birds.

Hunting on Goura spp

The main reason of hunting on *Goura* spp is to gain the cash money to meet daily needs of hunter's family. Hunted birds can be sold alive or in the form of smoked meat. However, it was found that hunters from Buare and Dabra villages in Mamberamo region usually sell fresh wildmeat in local market (Keiluhu, 2013). In some cases, hunters are asked by people from cities to provide and sell birds alive as pets (Pangau-Adam, pers. observation). For that reason, Goura should be captured without having injuries. Hunters and their family also consume the bird's meat as protein source, although it might be occurred very rarely, because they prefer to sell the birds.

Unlike hunting of Bird of Paradise which is mainly for collecting bird's feathers, *Goura* spp were rarely hunted for their beautiful feathers especially the crowns. The Victoria crowned pigeon and other *Goura* species are the most striking members of the pigeon family. The combination of their large size body with unique crowns, coloration and appearance makes them attractive for prized collections. Victoria crowned-pigeon *Goura Victoria* and its relatives are known as the high-valued bird at national and international level. Hence, these magnificent birds are also popular and highly prized as an aviary bird for the bird parks, zoos and private aviculturists throughout the world (Wetzel, 1992).

Traditionally in many forest areas in New Guinea, hunting on *Goura* spp and cassowaries are undertaken by men including youths. In several local communities they determined it as the man-fully activity. Sometimes, other family members including children should join hunting trips if the forest destination are far from the village and hunting trip may take several days (Keiluhu, 2013). Hunters usually build simple huts in the forest to rest during hunting trips (Pangau-Adam, pers. observation). Although the wifes are allowed to join hunting trips, they should stay around the huts to look after their children, collect wild vegetables, and fish in small ponds and creeks around their huts while waiting. In Mamberamo region, during hunting trips women would run sago harvesting and collecting wild vegetables in forest site near hunting huts (Boissiére *et al.* 2007). In this area, only men including young men are considered to absolutely know about the traditional forests and hunting boundaries between tribes and between villages. This seems to be similar with another study in New Guinea Highlands, where the women were never observed pacing through with hunting weapons and equipments or going into the forest for hunting practices (Silitoe, 2001).

Conclusion and recommendation

Wildlife hunting in Indonesian New Guinea has been practiced since many years for livelihood and also for socio-cultural reasons. In the faced of globalization and transition, the pattern of wildlife hunting in this region is gradually changed from subsistence level to the commercial purposes. Due to their body size, large ground dwelling birds such as cassowaries and *Goura* spp are specifically targeted by hunters and bird traders. Continued illegal hunting and bird trade to fulfil international demands may inevitably cause the population decline of these birds and furthermore lead to extirpation. The law enforcement and strict control on wildlife hunting and bird trade are therefore crucial to reduce illegal hunting activities in Indonesian New

Guinea. Moreover, sustainable hunting management of non-native species such as wild pigs and rusa deer might be an alternative approach to protect endemic fauna in New Guinea rainforests.

References

Aiyadurai, A., N.J. Singh & E.J. Milner-Gulland. 2010. Wildlife hunting by indigenous tribes: a case study from Arunachal Pradesh, North-east India. Oryx 44 (4): 564–572

Aiyadurai, A. 2011. Wildlife hunting and conservation in northeast India: a need for an interdisciplinary understanding. International Journal of Galliformes Conservation 2: 61–73.

Bennett, E.L. and J.G. Robinson, 2000. Hunting for sustainability: The start of synthesis. In: Hunting for sustainable in tropical forest, eds. J.G. Robinson, and E.L. Bennett. 499–520. New York. Columbia University Press.

BirdLife International, 2012. Threatened Birds of Asia: the Bird Life International Red Data Book. BirdLife International, Cambridge. http://www.birdlife.org/datazone/info/spcasrdb (accessed 31October 2012).

Boissiére, M., N. Liswanti, M. Padmanaba & D. Sheil, 2007. People priorities and perception-towards conservation partnership in Mamberamo. Center for International Forests Research. http://www.cifor.org/mla/download/publication/People%20priorities.pdf (accessed April 9, 2012).

Conservational International, 1999. The Irian Jaya biodiversity conservation priority-setting workshop, Biak, 7 –12 January 1997. Final Report. Washington, D.C., Conservation International.

Crome, H.J. & L.A. Moore, 1990. Cassowaries in north-eastern Queensland: report of a survey and a review and assessment of their status and conservation and management needs. AustralianWildlife Research, 17, 369–385.

Cuthbert, R. 2010. Sustainability of Hunting, Population Densities, Intrinsic Rates of Increase and Conservation of Papua New Guinean Mammals: A Quantitative Review. Biological Conservation 1438: 1850–1859.

Dwyer, P.D. and M. Minnegal. 1991. Hunting in lowland, tropical rain forest: towards a model of non agricultural subsistence. Human Ecology 19 (2): 187–212.

King, C.E. and J. Nijboer. 1994. Conservation Consideration for Ground Pigeons, genus Goura. Oryx 28 (1): 22–30

Government Regulation, 1998. Peraturan Pemerintah RI No. 68 Tentang Kawasan Suaka Alam dan Kawasan Pelestarian Alam. Pemerintah, Indonesia.

Johnson, A., Bino R. & P. Igag, 2004. A preliminary evaluation of the sustainability of cassowary (Aves: Casuariidae) capture and trade in Papua New Guinea. Animal Conservation, 7, 129–137.

Keiluhu, H.J., 2013. The impact of hunting on victoria crowned pigeon (*Goura victoria*: Columbidae) in the rainforests of northern Papua, Indonesia. Dissertation, eDiss, University of Gottingen, Germany.

Kwapena, N. 1984. Traditional conservation and utilization of wildlife in Papua New Guinea. The Environmentalist 4: 22–26.

Lee, R. J. 2000. Impact of subsistence hunting in north Sulawesi, Indonesia and conservation option. In: Robinson, J.G. & E.L. Benneth (Eds.) Hunting for sustainable in tropical forest. Columbia University Press. New York. Pp. 455–472.

Mack, A.L. & J. Dumbacher, 2007. Birds of Papua. In: The Ecology of Papua Part One, eds. A.J. Marshall and B. Beehler. 654–688. Singapore. Periplus Edition.

Mack, A. L., & P. West, 2005. Ten thousand tonnes of small animals: wildlife consumption in Papua New Guinea, a vital resource in need of management. Resource Management in Asia-Pacific Working Paper No. 61. Resource Management in Asia-Pacific Program, Research School of Pacific and Asian Studies, Australian National University, Canberra.

Majnep, I. S., & R. Bulmer, 1977. Birds of my Kalam Country.Aukland University Press, Aukland.

Noss, A., 2000. Cable snares and nets in the Central African Republic. In: Hunting for Sustainable in Tropical Forest, eds. J.G. Robinson and E.L. Bennett. 282–304. New York. Columbia University Press.

Pangau-Adam, M. & R. Noske, 2010. Wildlife Hunting and Bird Trade in Northern Papua. In: Ethno-ornithology: Global studies in Indigenous ornithology, culture, society and conservation, Eds. Tidemann, S., Gosler, A. and R. Gosford, Earthscan, London, pp 73–85.

Pangau-Adam, M., Noske, R. & M. Mühlenberg, 2012. Wildmeat or Bushmeat? Subsistence hunting and commercial harvesting in Papua, Indonesia. Human Ecology   40: 611-621.

Pangau-Adam, M. & M. Muehlenberg, 2014. Palm seeds in the diet of of the northern cassowary (*Casuarius unappendiculatus*) in Jayapura region, Papua, Indonesia.Palms 58: 19–26.

Pangau-Adam, M., Mühlenberg, M. & M. Waltert, 2015. Rainforest disturbance affects population density of the northern cassowary *Casuarius unappendiculatus* in Papua, Indonesia. Oryx 49: 735–742.

Pattiselanno, F. 2003. The wildlife value: example from West Papua, Indonesia. Tiger Paper 30 (1):27–29.

Petocz, R.G., 1978. Conservation and Development in Irian Jaya. A Strategy for Rational Resource Utilization. Leiden. E.J. Brill.

Petocz, R., 1989. Conservation and Development in Irian Jaya. E.J. Brill. Leiden PrincetonUniversity Press, New Jersey.

Pratt T.K., & B. Beehler, 2015. The Birds of New Guinea. New York Princeton University Press.

Richards, S. J. & S. Suryadi, 2000. A Biodiversity Assessment of Yongsu – Cyclop Mountains and the Southern Mamberamo basin, Papua. RAP Bulletin of Biological Assessment 25. Conservation International, Washington DC.

Sillitoe, P., 2001. Hunting for Conservation in Papua-New Guinea Highlands. Ethnos 66: 365–393.

Stattersfield, A. J., Crosby, N. J., Long, A. G., & C. Wege, 1998. Endemic Bird Areas of the World. Priority Areas for Biodiversity Conservation. Birdlife Conservation Series no. 7. Birdlife International, Cambridge.

Sujatnika. P. Jepson, T.R. Suhartono, M.J. Cosby and A. Mardiastuti, 1995. Melestarikan keanekaragaman hayati Indonesia: pendekatan Daerah burung endemik (Conservation biodiversity of Indonesia: approaches of endemic bird area). Jakata. Directorate of Forest Protection and Nature Conservation. BirdLife International Indonesia Programme.

Wetzel, 1992. The crowned pigeons. Bulletion of Kansas City Zoological Gardens pp. 30–34.

Greenhouse Farm Effects on Nutrient Levels and pH Content in a Peatland: The Case of Ondiri Swamp, Kenya

EVA NTARA

University of Bayreuth, Germany

Email: Eva.Ntara@uni-bayreuth.de

Abstract

Peatlands occur in different landscapes and have a naturally accumulated peat layer at the surface, whereas peat is the surface organic layer of a soil consisting of partially decomposed organic material, derived mostly from plants. Local communities often depend on peatlands (as with most other wetlands) and their inherent ecosystem services for their livelihoods. However, peatlands are often degraded under different land use types or threatened by future development. This paper seeks to analyze the effects of greenhouse farming activities on nutrient and pH content on Ondiri Swamp in Kikuyu, Kenya. The results indicate that analyzing peatland vegetation patterns, drainage intensity and land use patterns is crucial to understand the health status of the peatland ecosystems and the degree of disturbance by different land use management practices.

Key words: Peatlands, land use, local communities, ecosystem services, Ondiri swamp

Introduction

Kenya is located in East Africa and has an area of 582,646 km^2 (Microsoft Encarta Encyclopaedia 2002). The country is endowed by an array of internal wetlands dispersed around its six water basins: Lake Victoria North, Lake Victoria South, Rift Valley, Ewaso Ng'iro, Tana and Athi (Businge et al. 2012) as designated by the Water Resources Management Authority (WRMA). Some of the wetlands within these basins play such important ecological roles that they have been classified designated as Wetlands of International Importance (Ramsar Sites). Despite of this, many areas are increasingly degrading due to land use changes – especially peatland ecosystems.

Previous research confirmed the occurrence of peatlands in Kenya in the Kaisungor swamp (South West Cherangani Hills; Coetzee 1967), in the Karimu mire (Aberdare Ranges; Perrot & Street 1982), at Mount Elgon (on the Kenyan/Ugandan border; Shrier 1985), and in the Ondiri Swamp (Kiambu County; Ogondo 2008). Markov et al. (1988) estimates the area of 'peat resources' in Kenya as being 1,000 km^2, whereas D'Costa et al. (1994) mentions a 'probable peatland' area of 1,600 km^2, consisting of histosols and swampland soils, with 20–30% organic matter. When peatlands are drained, huge amounts of carbon dioxide (CO_2) are released making them important for climate change mitigation. Undrained peatlands provide manifold ecosystem services such as water regulation, flood control, biodiversity conservation, and carbon sequestration (Schumann & Joosten 2008).

The plants growing on a peatland shape their habitat in a unique way as they form peat as their growth substrate. Peatland vegetation changes gradually because of the origin of water that feeds it, acidity levels (pH), availability of main nutrients (nitrogen and phosphorus), water table level and depth of the peat (Aapala et al. 2012). Ondiri swamp occurs within the Athi Basin and is mainly used by the local farmers around the region as a source of water for their crops. The water is pumped or channeled using generators and drainage ditches respectively from the swamp and abstracted for use in the greenhouse and small-scale farms. After application of fertilizers within the greenhouse farms, the water that becomes rich in fertilizers is drained back into the swamp. Hence the goals of this paper are (1) To assess the effects of the greenhouse farms on the nutrient-level and pH in the swamp and (2) To analyze how the nutrient and pH levels influence vegetation composition in the peatland.

Study Area

Ondiri swamp is characterized by bog-like characteristics and covers an area of approximately 30 hectares (Macharia et al. 2010). The swamp is located at latitude 1°15′ and longitude 36°40′ in Kikuyu division in Central Province, Kenya. The area of the swamp is approximately 468,000 square meters and it lies in a depression-like landscape feature. The swamp is believed to be the second largest quacking bog in Africa and the source of Nairobi River and Lake Naivasha. The area has an average yearly temperature of 26°C. The low temperatures are experienced during the months of July and August whereas the hottest months are normally March, February and January. The rainfall pattern is usually bimodal with short rains happening during October and November and long rains occurring in April and May. The average rainfall amount that falls per year is 1500mm (Ogondo 2008). The fluctuations in temperature and rainfall are influenced by the monsoonal systems of Asia and the Indian Ocean that play an integral role in the existence and composition of Ondiri Swamp.

Figure 1. Ondiri Swamp, Kikuyu

The peat composition contains numerous species of Cyparaceae, reeds, water grass, typha, *Biden pilosa, Sphaeranthus gomphrenoides, Melanthera scandens* and *Oxygonium sinuatum,* that grow around the swamp (Macharia et al. 2010). The plants grow continuously to produce a huge amount of organic matter that accumulates and decomposes slowly on the surface of the swamp to form a thick mat (Figure 2), approximately 50cm thick (Ogondo 2008). The peat is stable enough to accommodate the weight of a human being. The soils found in and around the area are organic soils that are normally well-drained and extremely dark to reddish brown clay.

Figure 2. Peat Mat Growing on Ondiri Swamp

Land Uses around the Swamp

The major land uses in the area are agriculture, settlements and wetlands (Figure 3). The activities in the wetland involve abstraction of water for irrigation and domestic uses that are geared towards commercial or subsistence production. There are water pumps around the swamp that are not metered, so make it impossible to gauge the level of water abstraction. There is a mix of residential plots, large farms, small gardens and exotic vegetation around Ondiri swamp. Because of the proximity of the swamp to Kikuyu town and the capital city Nairobi, farmers prefer to practice horticultural production and take advantage of the good transport system networks (Ogondo, 2008). The swamp provides scenic views and is often used as a recreational site or meditation area by most locals. Due to the lack of ownership of the swamp, the wetland suffers from the concept of the 'tragedy of commons' that continues to threaten the sensitive ecosystem into loss of biodiversity and proper functioning of the peatland in terms of carbon storage.

(1)

(2)

(3)

(4)

Figure 3. (1) Greenhouse farms (2) Bee Farms. (3) Settlements located at a higher elevation above the swamp. (4) Green pepper being produced in a greenhouse

Methodology

After taking a reconnaissance visit to the swamp, the study area was chosen in a region of the swamp where the major land use practice is agriculture. There are greenhouses growing tomatoes and green pepper and next to them are local farmers practicing small-scale subsistence production of crops such as bananas, maize and vegetables. Eight different sites (A-H) near the greenhouses and small-scale farms were identified at the edge of the swamp where there were different vegetation types growing on the peat. Basic information on the physical features of the study area (relief, water supply, geology, etc.) was collected through literature review. Remote Sensing was essential in identifying temporal variations in land use and vegetation patterns. The study was carried out through zig-zag sampling method on the two sites; Greenhouse farms (Site 1: A, B, C, D points) and Small-Scale farms (Site 2: E, F, G, H points). Ground truthing was carried out to verify land use and vegetation patterns observed through Remote Sensing. The GPS points of the peat coring was transferred to a GIS environment.

Figure 4. Sample Collection Points (A-H)

Peat samples were collected by use of a specialized peat auger up to a depth of 100 cm. Peat soils have been described as organic soils with dark colour, lighter weight and greasy touch as compared to mineral soils (Vepraskas & Craft, 2016). Only samples at the depth of 0–20 cm were collected in sample plastic bags for further laboratory analysis. Three replications were done at each point of both peat, water and vegetation samples. In accordance to the Water Resources Department (2009), Nitrogen was measured by Alkaline Permanganate method, Phosphorus by Olsen Method, and Potassium by Flame Photometer Method. The pH level was measured in the field by use of a pH meter and recorded.

Results

The raw data obtained was analyzed through SPSS Statistics Software to obtain group statistics, independent sample T tests and a Levine's Test for equality of variances of the treatments. The percentage values and histogram charts were derived for each of the variables (see Figures 5 & 6); Nitrogen, Potassium, Phosphorus and pH. There was a significant difference (p= 0.009) value in Nitrogen content from the samples collected in all the areas showing that it affected the vegetation composition whereas the other parameters such as Phosphorus, Potassium and pH content had no significant difference due to their p values; Phosphorus (p=0.949), Potassium (p=0.390) and pH (p=0.158).

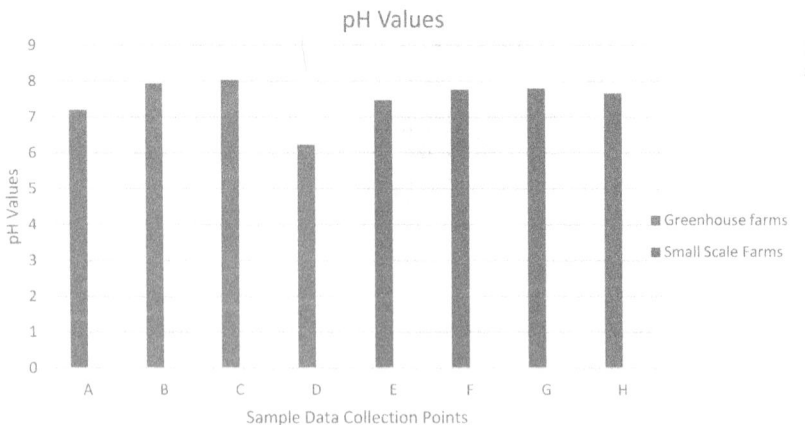

Figure 5. The pH values of sampling points

NPK CONTENT

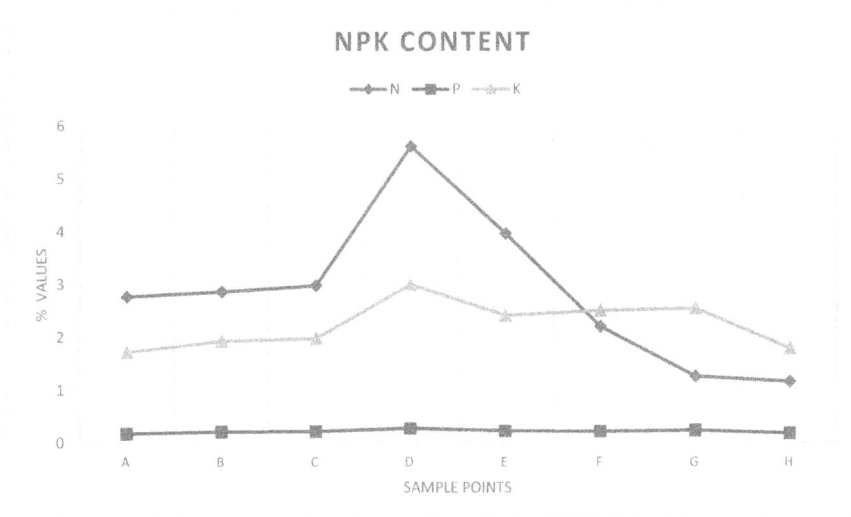

Figure 6. NPK Content Values of Sampling Points

Table 1, Vegetation Species found at the sampling points

Sampling point	Plant name
A	*Portulaca oleracea*
B	*Lactuca serriola*
C	*Cyperus sp.*
D	*Portulaca oleracea*
E	*Water Grass (Vossia)*
F	*Typha Cattalis*
G	*Reeds*
H	*Water Grass (Vossia)*

Discussion

The site (**1**) under Green-houses had a significant impact on the nutrient levels in the swamp. When compared with site (**2**) under small-scale farming, site (**1**) had higher significant values of Nitrogen levels. For both sites (**1**) and (**2**), the pH values did not have any significant effect on the water quality. Hence, the main assumption is that pH values of the water may not be affected by input of fertilizers from the Greenhouse farms at Ondiri swamp. In terms of vegetation composition, it was noted that nitrogen levels have a direct effect on the occurrence of invasive species at the edge of the swamp. The occurrence of the weeds *Portulaca oleracea* and *Lactula serriola* signify the high presence of Nitrogen content in the swamp. Previous research has revealed that these specific weeds are usually located in disturbed wetland ecosystems. However, the other nutrient parameters such as Potassium and Phosphorus were noted to have an insignificant effect on the vegetation composition of the swamp.

Conclusion

It was generally noted that agricultural fertilizers rich in nitrogen had a significant effect on the vegetation composition in the swamp through the introduction of invasive weed species that thrive in nitrogen- rich conditions. Notably, the site area (**1**) under Green-house farms had more invasive vegetation species as compared to the small-scale farms on site (**2**). Consequently, invasive vegetation species in a peatland alters peat composition that directly impacts on the peat decomposition rate and carbon storage capacity. Ondiri Swamp is a classic example of the tragedy of the commons phenomenon whereby there is unregulated land uses around it that exposes to water abstraction and poor water quality that affects the peat quality. An integrated peatland management framework for peatlands in the region can generate multiple benefits such as local community empowerment, sustainable ecosystem services, biodiversity conservation and climate protection.

References

Aapala, K.S. R., 2012. Peatland Biodiversity. Ireland: International Peat Society.

Awuor, O. J., 2008. Paleoclimate of Ondiri Swamp,Kikuyu,Kenya. (Doctoral dissertation, University of Nairobi).

Businge M. S., 2012. Kenya wetlands atlas. Nairobi Kenya: Ministry of Environment and Mineral Resources.

Joosten, H. and Clarke, D. 2002. Wise use of mires and peatlands – Background and principles including a framework for decision-making. International Peat Society.

Macharia, J, T. T.. 2012. Management of highland wetlands in central Kenya:the importance of community education, awareness and eco-tourism in biodiversity conservation. 85– 90.

Perrott, R. A., & F.A. Street-Perrott, 1982. New evidence for a late Pleistocene wet phase in northern intertropical Africa. Palaeoecology of Africa, 14, 57–75.

Schumann M. & H. Joosten, 2008. Global Peatland Restoration Manual. Available at: http://www.imcg.net/media/download_gallery/books/gprm_01.pdf, checked on 2/28/2019.

Vepraskas, M.J., & C.B. Craft, 2016. Wetland Soils: Genesis, Hydrology, Landscapes, and Classification (Second Edition). Boca Raton, Florida, U.S.A., London, U.K. and New York, New York, USA, CRC Press.

Water Resources Department, 2009. Laboratory Testing Procedure for soil and water sample analysis.